APPLE
KITCHEN

Madeleine and Florian Ankner

APPLE
KITCHEN

Contents

When we were kids, growing up in Germany, the apple trees in our grandparents' garden were far more than just plants. In spring and summer, we transformed the trees into adventure playgrounds, throwing sheets around the branches and creating robbers' dens. We climbed right to the top, stealing the first fruit straight from the tree, or we spread out our picnic blanket under the leafy green canopy to enjoy a huge piece of granny's freshly baked apple strudel at harvest time.

Our days of building dens and climbing trees are behind us—but the happy memories remain. And no doubt this fueled our desire to devote an entire book to this wonderful fruit and to showcase just how versatile the apple can be. Sweet, tangy, fruity, tart: each variety has its own unique flavor and adds something special to all sorts of different recipes.

As well as popular and modern varieties, we have included some of the older apple varieties, such as

Preface

The sight of an apple brings back the loveliest childhood memories: climbing trees, biting into juicy fruit, and enjoying life.

Cortland and Northern Spy, which date from the 19th century. There are varieties that have been cultivated, harvested, and eaten for many centuries, but have gradually been neglected or even completely forgotten by consumers. Roughly 20,000 varieties are recognized, but only a couple of dozen have any economic significance.

Apples have taken us on a culinary voyage. This began back in 2013 when we started our food blog "Das Backstübchen" ("the little bakery"), which is indebted to the baking skills passed down by Madeleine's grandmother. Her recipes continue to inspire us today. Best of all is her delicious apple strudel, which we have included in this book along with other classics from our childhood, such as baked apples, apple fritters, and Florentine apple cake.

We seek out culinary inspiration from other countries with tarte tatin, pierogi, and clams cooked in cider. We deploy the apple in all its different guises—sometimes fruity and sweet, other times tart and acidic; sometimes we use the whole fruit, other times the purée or juice. It never ceases to amaze us how beautifully the scent and taste of the apple blends in with savory dishes and ingredients, as well as sweet.

We hope our culinary creations will also inspire you to a new appreciation for our favorite fruit, while bringing back some lovely childhood memories in the process.

INTRODUCTION

The roots of the modern apple

Melting snow forms little lakes and a biting wind streams over the mountain ridge, which is among the highest in the world. On the slopes, the treetops are a brilliant yellow and red. Here, in southeast Kazakhstan, is the Garden of Eden—where the apple finds its origins.

The birthplace of the apple is close to the mighty Tian Shan mountains and the former Kazakh capital city of Almaty, which translates as "father of apples." A glance at the surrounding slopes quickly explains where the name originates: huge numbers of apple trees grow in small woodlands, entirely wild and natural, seeded without human intervention. The apples here are very different from the fruit we know today. In terms of size and appearance, they are more akin to cherries. It is immediately obvious that a lot had to happen before the apple would become one of Europe's favorite fruits.

Because these Asian crab apples were extremely small and woody, with lots of seeds and a very sour flavor, people used them as fodder for wild horses and deer. The animals distributed the seeds through their dung. In ancient times, people began taking specimens into the Black Sea region via the Silk Road. Different varieties were crossed with each other, and scientific research has shown that today's apples have traces of at least four wild apple varieties.

The apple was eventually cultivated by the Romans and Greeks and was introduced to Central and Northern Europe by Roman legions around 100 BCE. The fruit tasted sweeter by this point—and it was credited with special properties. The Greeks even believed the apple could work as an aphrodisiac. In the Holy Roman Empire, the apple symbolized the globe and was held in the ruler's left hand as a kind of imperial orb during coronation ceremonies. Over the millennia, apples have been a symbol of power, wealth, and temptation.

Today, the apple is an everyday product. And its agricultural significance has steadily increased too: by 1880, it is thought that more than 20,000 varieties of apples were being cultivated around the world. However, as the fruit-growing business was commercialized, only a few varieties with the highest yield were economically viable.

According to the US Apple Association, the main apples currently being cultivated in the United States are Gala and Red Delicious. These are followed by Granny Smith, Fuji, Honeycrisp, and Golden Delicious. Nowadays, apples are grown using a space-saving tall spindle system. Trees are grown to 10 feet tall on trellises, but have small trunks and no scaffold branches. This maximizes yield. The fruit are geared toward USDA standards and the requirements of the retail trade: they must be crisp and juicy and have good storage and transportation characteristics.

The responsibility for preserving older apple varieties now falls mainly to specialized associations. If you want to promote diversity, you should buy regional produce and seek out unusual varieties or plant your own heirloom apple tree in your garden.

1 | IDARED

2 | GALA

4 | PINK LADY

3 | CORTLAND

5 | MCINTOSH

6 | HONEYCRISP

Apple varieties

1 | IDARED

Season: end of September to January

Flavor: sweet, tangy, and very juicy

Ideal use: because they hold their shape so nicely, Idareds are the perfect baked apple. They also make excellent apple butter, jelly, and sauce

Characteristic: developed in Idaho, Idared apples are a cross between two New York varieties, Jonathan and Wagener. They make a beautiful pink-hued applesauce if cooked with the skins on.

2 | GALA

Season: May to September

Flavor: juicy flesh with a sweet taste

Ideal use: typical dessert apple, popular with children thanks to its low acidity and sweet flavor

Characteristic: Gala is one of the most popular apples in the US.

3 | CORTLAND

Season: September to December

Flavor: a zesty apple with subtle spice and a good dose of acidity

Ideal use: due to its hints of nutmeg and spice, Cortland is a great apple for crisps, crumbles, tarts, and pies

Characteristic: an older American variety and one of many offsprings of the McIntosh apple.

4 | PINK LADY

Season: October to July

Flavor: crisp bite and zippy flavor with an effervescent finish

Ideal use: very versatile, and popular both in fruit salads and desserts. Superb for baking into cakes or just slicing and snacking

Characteristic: the high acid content means these apples are slow to oxidize (turn brown), making them perfect for cheese boards or fruit salads.

5 | MCINTOSH

Season: July to November

Flavor: a super juicy bite with a tart finish, and that iconic spiced-cider flavor

Ideal use: the preferred apple for applesauce, but it is also great for juicing, making cider, or cooking with roast meats

Characteristic: McIntosh apples were grown long before the emergence of the personal computer, but as Macintosh developer Jef Raskin's favorite apple, they became the inspiration for the name of the original Apple desktop.

6 | HONEYCRISP

Season: year round

Flavor: large, sweet, juicy, and extremely refreshing

Ideal use: Honeycrisps are the ideal cheese-board apple. They cut into firm slices, which also makes them excellent in salads but not so good for baking. Save them for snacking or savory dishes

Characteristic: this extremely popular apple almost never came to be. When first developed by the University of Minnesota it was thrown in the discard pile, but a young researcher, David Bedford, decided to give it another chance and the rest is history.

7 | BRAEBURN

Season: October to April

Flavor: firm and crisp with a slightly tart but sweet taste

Ideal use: as a dessert apple, but also good in salads

Characteristic: the New Zealand Braeburn was the first two-colored apple to be sold internationally.

8 | JONAGOLD

Season: September to October

Flavor: juicy, sweet apple with low acidity; it has a floral aroma

Ideal use: suitable for baking, purée, compote, cakes, or preserving

Characteristic: the Jonagold is a very young apple. It was cultivated in 1943 in the United States and is a cross between the Golden Delicious and Jonathan apples.

9 | GRANNY SMITH

Season: September to October

Flavor: tart flavor

Ideal use: typical dessert apple, also tastes great in sorbet and ice cream or with fish

Characteristic: this apple has a long ripening time of 150 days and it needs a warm climate. Most Granny Smiths in the US are grown in central Washington, where there is ample sunshine.

10 | FUJI

Season: October to December

Flavor: predominantly sweet with a faint hint of tartness at the end, juicy, and crunchy

Ideal use: the ultimate snacking apple, perfect for slicing into salads or stacking on sandwiches. Its firm texture also makes it excellent for dipping

Characteristic: a hybrid of a Red Delicious and a Ralls Janet, two American breeds. Nowadays it is grown all over Europe.

11 | NORTHERN SPY

Season: October to November

Flavor: creamy white, crisp, and mildly sweet with a heady fragrance

Ideal use: commonly used for desserts and pies, but just as good as an eating apple, and popular with cider makers

Characteristic: these large apples streaked with red and yellow were first cultivated in Bloomfield, New York around 1800. They are a hearty apple and grow well in colder climates, hence the name.

12 | GOLDEN DELICIOUS

Season: September to October

Flavor: sweet apple with low acidity

Ideal use: suitable as a dessert apple, for baking, purée, or juicing

Characteristic: hybrids based on the Golden Delicious include many well-known varieties such as Pink Lady, Jonagold, and Gala. This is the most widely cultivated variety in the world.

Note: *Most varieties of apples are available year-round in the US due to cold storage and imports from the Southern Hemisphere.*

8 | JONAGOLD

7 | BRAEBURN

9 | GRANNY SMITH

10 | FUJI

12 | GOLDEN DELICIOUS

11 | NORTHERN SPY

APPETIZERS AND SNACKS

Kale salad with apples and marinated squash

Serves 4
Preparation 30 minutes

For the squash
about 1lb 9oz (700g)
    butternut squash,
    unpeeled or peeled
1 tbsp butter
2 tsp honey
¼ cup olive oil
¼ cup white balsamic
    vinegar
2 tsp dukkah (North African
    spice mix; alternatively
    2 tsp curry powder)
salt and freshly ground
    black pepper

For the salad dressing
1 garlic clove
3 tbsp tahini
2 tbsp full-fat yogurt
2 tsp honey
salt and freshly ground
    black pepper

For the salad
16 stems of kale
    (about 1lb 5oz/600g)
2 tbsp olive oil
1 red onion
1 avocado
2 apples (e.g. Jonagold, Gala,
    McIntosh)
¼ cup almonds
1 tsp sesame seeds

Wash the squash and peel it if you prefer. Remove the seeds and stringy fibers. Chop into slices roughly ½in (1cm) thick, then cut large pieces into halves or thirds. Melt the butter in a griddle pan and grill the squash, or sauté in a regular pan for 10 minutes. Remove from the stove and leave to cool slightly.

Meanwhile, combine the honey, oil, vinegar, and dukkah in a bowl for the marinade and season with salt and pepper. Add the sliced squash to a bowl and drizzle with the marinade. Leave the flavors to infuse for 20–30 minutes.

Peel and crush the garlic. Combine with the tahini, yogurt, honey, and 2 tablespoons of water to make the dressing.

Season with salt and pepper. Wash the kale, let it drain well, cut out any thick veins in the leaves, and tear into bite-sized pieces. Mix the leaves with the olive oil in a bowl and massage with your hands for 2–3 minutes until the kale feels soft.

Slice the onion into thin rings. Peel and pit the avocado and cut the flesh into cubes. Core the apples and then slice or cube them. Roughly chop the almonds. Add everything to the kale along with the dressing and toss together well. Finally, add the squash and sprinkle the salad with sesame seeds.

Salad with apple, goat cheese balls, and a honey mustard vinaigrette

Serves 4
Preparation 25 minutes

For the vinaigrette
1 shallot
¼ cup olive oil
6 tbsp white balsamic vinegar
1½ tbsp honey
2 tbsp mustard
salt and freshly ground
    black pepper

For the salad
1½–2 apples (e.g. Pink Lady,
    Honeycrisp, Jonagold)
1–1½ beets, cooked
400g (14oz) mixed green
    salad leaves
1 handful of tender shoots,
    such as pea, broccoli,
    lentil, or mung bean
3 tbsp sesame seeds
3 tbsp chia seeds
5½oz (150g) roll of soft goat
    cheese, cut into 12 rounds

To make the vinaigrette, finely chop the shallot. Heat the oil in a small pan and sauté the shallot until translucent. Deglaze with balsamic vinegar, remove from the stove, and leave to cool. Stir in the honey and mustard, and season with salt and pepper.

To make the salad, quarter and core the apples, and then cut them into slices. Strain the beets if necessary and slice. Wash the salad leaves and shoots and shake them dry. Put the sesame seeds and chia seeds into separate small bowls. Shape the goat's cheese rounds with your hands to make 12 balls, and roll them in the sesame seeds and chia seeds until coated. Toss the salad with the vinaigrette and serve with sliced apple, beets, shoots, and goat cheese balls.

Bulgur wheat is one of the main ingredients in Middle Eastern cuisine, where it is traditionally prepared with parsley, mint, and tomatoes to make tabbouleh. We serve our bulgur salad with cucumber, feta, almonds, and tart apples.

Apple and bulgur salad with fresh herbs and feta

Serves 4
Preparation 25 minutes

For the salad
½ cup bulgur wheat
1½ cups vegetable stock
2 medium sweet and tangy
    apples (e.g. Pink Lady,
    Cortland, Jonagold)
1 small cucumber
1 small bunch of fresh
    cilantro
1 small bunch of flat-leaf
    parsley
2 sprigs of mint
¼ cup almonds
5½oz (150g) feta cheese

For the dressing
½ tsp fennel seeds
zest and juice of 1
    organic lemon
3 tbsp olive oil
1 tbsp vinegar
2½ tbsp apple juice
½ tsp cumin
½ tbsp honey (optional)
salt and freshly ground
    black pepper

Put the bulgur wheat in a sieve and rinse until the water runs clear. Transfer to a pan, add the stock, and bring to a boil. Turn down the heat, cover, and simmer for 7–10 minutes. Remove from the stove and leave to cool, stirring frequently during this time.

Wash, core, and cut the apples into cubes. Peel and cube the cucumber. Wash and shake dry the herbs, and remove the mint leaves from the stalks. Roughly chop the herbs and the almonds. Mash the feta with a fork.

To make the dressing, crush the fennel seeds in a pestle and mortar. Put the lemon zest and juice into a bowl. Add the fennel seeds, oil, vinegar, apple juice, cumin, and honey, if using. Season to taste with salt and pepper.

Put the cooled bulgur wheat into a large bowl with the herbs, apples, cucumber, and dressing, and mix well. Leave the flavors to infuse and, if necessary, adjust the seasoning. Before serving, add the feta and scatter over the almonds.

In Bavaria, traditional bread platters are always served with a radish salad in an oil and vinegar dressing. We've enhanced the classic recipe with the addition of some crunchy Honeycrisps or Granny Smiths, which are excellent in salads thanks to their tangy and slightly bitter flavor.

Apple and radish salad

Serves 4
Preparation 15 minutes
Resting 1 hour

For the salad
1lb 2oz (500g) daikon radish
    (mooli)
7oz (200g) pink radishes
    (about 8)
1 bunch of chives
1 bunch of dill
½ cup white balsamic
    vinegar
⅔ cup sunflower oil
1 tsp caraway seeds
2 tsp sugar
1 medium apple
    (e.g. Granny Smith,
    Honeycrisp)
salt and freshly ground
    black pepper

Peel the daikon radish and remove the ends. Use a mandoline or similar device to slice thinly. Wash the pink radishes and slice thinly with a sharp knife. Wash, shake dry, and finely chop the chives and dill.

Gradually add the balsamic vinegar, oil, caraway seeds, and sugar to the salad, mixing with a fork. Finally, leave the salad for at least 1 hour to allow the flavors to develop. Wash, quarter, and core the apple. Slice thinly and add to the salad. Season with salt and pepper.

Flo and I both agree—tarte flambée is one of our absolute favorites. You can vary the topping to suit your tastes and it doesn't take long to make. Our favorite is a crisp, sourdough tarte flambée topped with apple and crème fraîche, Parma ham and Roquefort. Make the dough the previous day and leave it to rest overnight in the fridge. This gives it a stronger flavor.

Tarte flambée with apple and crème fraîche, Parma ham, and Roquefort

Serves 4
Preparation 30 minutes
Cook 12 minutes
Resting 30 minutes–12 hours

For the tarte flambée
1 cup white spelt flour
½ tsp salt
1 tsp sugar
Scant 1oz (25g) sourdough starter (available online)
1 tbsp oil

For the topping
1¾oz (50g) arugula
2 sweet and tangy apples (e.g. Idared)
1 scallion
7fl oz (200ml) full-fat crème fraîche
1¾oz (50g) full-fat yogurt
salt and freshly ground black pepper
1 red onion
3 tbsp walnuts
3½oz (100g) Roquefort cheese
2¾oz (80g) Parma ham
olive oil for drizzling (optional)

To make the dough, combine the flour, salt, and sugar in a bowl. Add the sourdough starter, oil, and about ⅓ cup lukewarm water, and knead everything for 10 minutes until you have an elastic dough. If the dough is too sticky, gradually add a little more flour. Leave to rest for at least 30 minutes (or preferably overnight) in a bowl covered with a damp cloth.

Preheat the oven to 475°F (240°C). Put a pizza stone or upside-down baking tray in the oven on the bottom shelf.

For the topping, wash the arugula and apples. Slice the scallion into thin rings. Cut one apple into cubes and combine with the crème fraîche, yogurt, and scallion. Season with salt and pepper.

Finely slice the onion into half-moons. Roughly chop the walnuts. Slice the second apple into rings. Divide the Roquefort and Parma ham into four equal portions.

Divide the dough for the tarte flambée into four and roll each piece out into a thin disc on a floured work surface. Place each disc in turn on a floured pizza peel (paddle) or floured board, spread with crème fraîche, and top with apple slices and onion rings. Slide the discs onto the hot pizza stone or upturned baking tray and bake for 10–12 minutes until golden.

Remove from the oven and top with arugula, Roquefort, walnuts, and Parma ham, and drizzle with olive oil, if using.

It's time to consign boring sandwiches to history. We've taken this lunch-break classic and given it a modern twist—all with just a few ingredients.

Smoked trout sandwich with apple horseradish

Serves 4
Preparation 15 minutes

For the horseradish
1 Granny Smith apple
1¾oz (50g) fresh horseradish
¼ cup heavy cream
salt

For the sandwich
1¼oz (40g) arugula
4 pieces of rye baguette or
    4 slices of rye bread
9oz (250g) smoked trout
    fillets

Wash, quarter, and core the apple. Peel and finely grate the horseradish. Whip the cream until stiff. Grate half the apple and fold this into the whipped cream with the horseradish. Season with a pinch of salt.

Thinly slice the other apple half. Wash and shake dry the arugula.

Cut the baguette or rye slices in half and toast them. Spread half the slices with horseradish and top with the desired quantity of trout, sliced apple, and arugula. Top with the remaining slices of bread, and enjoy.

Pastrami is a beef speciality thought to have been introduced to the United States by Jewish immigrants toward the end of the 19th century. The meat is particularly delicate thanks to the special way it is prepared, cured, and smoked—and it tastes absolutely divine combined with cheese, apple, red cabbage, and apple mayonnaise.

Pastrami sandwiches with apple mayonnaise and red cabbage

Serves 4
Preparation 20 minutes

For the red cabbage
3½oz (100g) red cabbage
2 pinches of sugar
1 pinch of salt
1 sweet and tangy apple
(e.g. Pink Lady, Fuji,
Idared)

For the mayonnaise
1 medium egg yolk
1 tsp mustard
½ tsp white balsamic vinegar
(or cider vinegar)
½ cup neutral-flavored
vegetable oil (e.g.
sunflower or canola)
salt and freshly ground
black pepper

For the sandwich
4 or 8 slices of rye bread
(depending on size)
7oz (200g) pastrami
2¾oz (80g) Gruyère cheese,
thinly sliced
4 tsp apple butter
(optional; see p166)

Slice the red cabbage into thin strips. Add to a bowl with the sugar, and salt and toss everything with your hands. Halve and core the apple. Cube one of the halves and add to the red cabbage. Set the other half aside. Mix everything well and leave the flavors to infuse.

To make the apple mayonnaise, allow the egg yolk and oil to reach room temperature before using, otherwise they will not emulsify. Whisk the egg yolk, mustard, and balsamic vinegar in a bowl using a balloon whisk. Pour in the oil in a thin stream, whisking constantly until you have a thick, creamy mixture. Grate the remaining apple half, add to the mayonnaise, and season with salt and pepper.

Toast the slices of bread under the broiler or in a toaster until crisp. Cut large slices in half. In a pan, heat the pastrami slices on both sides, push them together, and top with the cheese. Leave in the pan until the cheese has melted. Spread half the slices of bread with mayonnaise and top with red cabbage and pastrami. Add some apple butter, if using, and top with the remaining slices of bread.

A warming soup does you a world of good in fall or winter. The curcumin contained in turmeric has an anti-inflammatory effect and also works as an antioxidant. The apple adds a fresh and tangy element to this soup.

Carrot and apple soup with turmeric and an apple and walnut topping

Serves 4
Preparation 35 minutes

For the soup
1lb 9oz (700g) carrots
1 onion
1 apple (e.g. Northern Spy)
1 garlic clove
Scant 1oz (25g) ginger
2 tbsp olive oil
1½ tsp ground turmeric
4¼ cups vegetable stock
⅔ cup heavy cream
salt and freshly ground
    black pepper

For the topping
⅓ cup walnuts
1 apple (e.g. Northern Spy)
2 tbsp butter
3 tbsp maple syrup
fine sea salt
1½ tsp thyme leaves
walnut oil for drizzling
pea shoots or beet shoots
    (optional)

Special equipment
blender
handheld blender

Chop the carrots into chunks and cube the onion. Peel, quarter, core, and roughly chop the apple. Peel and finely chop the garlic and ginger.

Heat the oil in a pan. Sauté the onion until translucent. Add the carrots and apples and continue frying for 2–3 minutes. Add the garlic, ginger, and turmeric and fry briefly. Pour in the vegetable stock and simmer for 20–25 minutes over a moderate heat until the carrots are soft. Remove the pan from the stove, pour in the cream, and blend the soup in a blender. Season with salt and pepper. Keep warm.

Roughly chop the walnuts for the topping. Wash, rub dry, quarter and core the apple then chop it

into large cubes. Melt the butter in a pan. Fry the apple and nuts in the butter for about 2 minutes. Add the maple syrup and allow to caramelize. Season with a pinch of sea salt and the thyme leaves. Remove from the stove.

To serve, heat the soup, use a handheld blender to make it slightly frothy, and pour into deep plates or bowls. Garnish with the apple and walnut topping, and drizzle with walnut oil. Add a few pea or beet shoots, if using.

Tip: to make a vegan version of the soup, just replace the butter with oil, and the heavy cream with coconut milk or oat or soy cream.

Leek and potato soup is a classic warming dish for fall and winter. Apple adds a fruity element to this savory soup.

Apple and leek soup

Serves 4
Preparation 30 minutes

For the soup
3½oz (100g) smoked
    pancetta
5½oz (150g) russet potatoes
1 garlic clove
1¾lb (800g) leeks
1 sweet and tangy apple
    (e.g. Braeburn, Fuji,
    Northern Spy)
2 tbsp butter
3 cups vegetable stock
½ cup heavy cream
salt and freshly ground
    black pepper
freshly grated nutmeg

For the topping
2 tbsp oil
3–4 apple chips
    (see p170)

Special equipment
blender

Roughly cut the pancetta into cubes. Peel and cube the potatoes, and peel and finely chop the garlic. Clean the leeks and slice into rings. Set aside around $^1/_3$ cup sliced leeks to use as a garnish. Peel, core, and cube the apple.

Melt the butter in a pan and fry the pancetta until crisp. Remove from the pan and set aside. Add the leeks, garlic, and potatoes to the pan, fry briefly, then add the vegetable stock and simmer until the potatoes are soft. Add the cubed apple and simmer briefly with the other ingredients. Blend the soup in a blender, add the cream, and season with salt, pepper, and nutmeg.

To make the topping, heat the oil in a pan. Fry the leeks you set aside for about 5 minutes until crisp, stirring occasionally. Serve the soup in deep plates or bowls and sprinkle with leeks, pancetta, and apple chips.

Ricotta and apple pierogi with Mediterranean pancetta in butter

Serves 4
Preparation 45–50 minutes
Resting 30 minutes

For the dough
1½ cups white spelt flour
1 medium egg
1 tsp oil
1 tsp salt

For the filling
1 tart apple (e.g. Fuji)
a little lemon juice for
    drizzling
7oz (200g) ricotta cheese
¾oz (20g) arugula
¼ cup walnuts, plus
    extra to garnish
salt and freshly ground
    black pepper

For the pancetta
4½oz (120g) smoked
    pancetta
7 tbsp butter
4 sprigs thyme, plus extra
    to garnish
4 sprigs rosemary, plus
    extra to garnish
salt and freshly ground
    black pepper

Sift the flour into a bowl. Whisk the egg and add to the flour along with the oil, salt, and ½ cup warm water. Knead for at least 10 minutes until you have a smooth and elastic dough. Shape into a ball, wrap in plastic wrap, and leave to rest at room temperature for about 30 minutes.

Meanwhile, prepare the filling. Wash and core the apple. Finely cube one half, drizzle with lemon juice, and set aside to use later. Finely grate the other half and stir into the ricotta. Wash, shake dry, and roughly chop the arugula. Likewise, roughly chop the walnuts, and add to the ricotta and apple filling along with the arugula. Season with salt and pepper.

Bring a pan of salted water to the boil. Roll out the dough in portions on a floured work surface until it is roughly ¹⁄₁₆–¹⁄₈in (2–4mm) thick, then cut out circles with a round cutter (roughly 4in/10cm in diameter). Put 1 teaspoon of the filling in the center of each piece of dough, moisten the edges with a little water, and fold the two sides together. Carefully press down the edges with a fork. Cover the finished pierogi with a cloth until ready to use. Simmer the little parcels in batches for about 2–3 minutes in salted water until they float to the surface. Scoop them out of the pan with a slotted spoon and drain in a sieve.

Slice the pancetta into strips roughly ¼in (5mm) wide. Melt the butter in a pan and add the pancetta, thyme, and rosemary. Season with salt and pepper and fry the pierogi in the butter for 5 minutes. Take care to avoid the parcels overlapping too much during frying. Deglaze the pan with 3 tablespoons of the pierogi cooking water.

Serve in deep plates, garnished with chopped walnuts, diced apple, and herbs.

We love all sorts of filled dumplings. So it's no surprise we are such big fans of pierogi. These little filled dumplings originated in Eastern Europe and can be made using pasta dough, leavened dough, or flaky pastry, and given a sweet or savory filling. In our version, a creamy apple and ricotta filling is beautifully complemented by Mediterranean-style pancetta in butter.

Baked apples are a winter and Christmas classic, but this savory version is also fantastic. Fruity apples are combined with salty bacon and feta. A topping made from crispy breadcrumbs and pomegranate seeds ensures a delicious crunch.

Baked apples stuffed with feta and bacon

Serves 4
Preparation 30 minutes
Cook 40 minutes

For the baked apples
4 apples, each about 7oz
　　(200g) (e.g. Fuji, Northern
　　Spy, McIntosh)
2¼oz (70g) bacon
3½oz (100g) feta cheese
3 tbsp walnuts
salt and freshly ground
　　black pepper
1 pinch ground cinnamon
1 pinch ground anise
4 sprigs thyme

For the topping
½ pomegranate
2 tbsp butter
2 tbsp sugar
3 tbsp plus 2 tsp raisins
¼ cup breadcrumbs

Wash and dry the apples. Cut off the tops to create lids and set them aside. Use a teaspoon to hollow out a large cavity in the apples. Preheat the oven to 400°F (200°C).

For the filling, roughly chop the bacon, feta, and walnuts, and combine in a bowl. Season with salt, pepper, cinnamon, and anise. Stuff the prepared apples with the filling, top each with a sprig of thyme, and arrange them side by side in an ovenproof casserole dish. Bake in the oven on the bottom shelf for 35–40 minutes. After about 20 minutes, put the lids on top of the apples and continue baking.

Meanwhile, remove the seeds from the pomegranate.

Melt the butter in a pan. Add the sugar, raisins, and breadcrumbs and sauté gently until golden, stirring constantly. Remove from the stove.

To serve, garnish the cooked apples with the breadcrumbs and pomegranate seeds.

Apple carpaccio with fennel gratin and a pomegranate vinaigrette

Serves 4
Preparation 20 minutes
Cook 20 minutes

For the fennel
1 fennel bulb
1 pinch ground anise
2 tbsp olive oil
1 tbsp white balsamic
    vinegar
juice of ¼ lemon
1 pinch sugar
¾oz (20g) Parmesan cheese,
    grated, plus extra shavings
    to garnish

For the vinaigrette
½ pomegranate
2 tbsp full-fat yogurt
1 tsp cider vinegar
1 tbsp olive oil
1 tsp honey
salt and freshly ground
    black pepper

For the carpaccio
2–3 sweet apples (e.g.
    McIntosh, Gala, Jonagold)
juice of ½ lemon
2¾–3½oz (80–100g) lamb's
    lettuce (corn salad)
1 scallion
nasturtium shoots (optional)
1 slice of bread of your
    choice
½ tbsp butter

Preheat the oven to 400°F (200°C/180°C). Wash and trim the fennel then cut into slices roughly ½in (1cm) thick. Stir the anise, oil, balsamic vinegar, lemon juice, and sugar together in a small bowl. Put the sliced fennel in an ovenproof dish, pour over the oil and vinegar marinade, and scatter the Parmesan on top. Bake in the oven on the middle shelf for about 20 minutes.

To make the vinaigrette, remove and set aside the seeds from the pomegranate and collect the juice. Combine the yogurt, vinegar, oil, honey, and pomegranate juice in a bowl. Season with salt and pepper.

Wash the apples and slice very thinly. Drizzle with lemon juice to stop them going brown. Wash the lamb's lettuce (corn salad), shake dry, and mix with the vinaigrette. Clean the scallion and slice into thin rings. Wash the nasturtium shoots, if using, and shake these dry too.

Cut the bread into cubes. Melt the butter in a pan and fry the bread cubes to make golden croutons.

Arrange the apple slices on plates and top with the fennel slices, lamb's lettuce, pomegranate seeds, and scallion, as well as the nasturtium shoots, if using. Drizzle with any remaining vinaigrette and garnish with the croutons and Parmesan shavings.

Tortillas with pulled chicken in an apple and tomato sauce

Serves 4
Preparation 50 minutes

For the chicken
1 onion
1 large sweet apple
   (e.g. Golden Delicious,
   McIntosh)
1 garlic clove
9oz (250g) chicken breast
⅔ cup hard cider
¼ cup white balsamic
   vinegar
2 tbsp oil
½ tsp salt
½ tsp pepper
½ tsp ground ginger
½ tsp ground cinnamon
1 tsp smoked ground paprika
1 tbsp tomato paste
⅓ cup tomato purée
   (from a jar)
1 tbsp maple syrup
chile flakes (optional)

For the tortillas
1 avocado
1 large sweet apple
   (e.g. Golden Delicious,
   McIntosh)
8 radishes
6–8 Padrón peppers (can
   substitute shishito
   peppers)
½ bunch of parsley
½ bunch of fresh cilantro
2 limes
8 flour tortillas (about
   8in/20cm in diameter)

Finely chop the onion. Peel, core, and roughly chop the apple. Peel the garlic. Add the chopped apple, chicken breast, garlic, cider, and balsamic vinegar to a pan. Bring to a boil, cover, and simmer for about 15 minutes.

Meanwhile, heat the oil in a small pan and sauté the onion until translucent. Add the salt, pepper, ginger, cinnamon, ground paprika, and tomato paste. Sauté for about 5 minutes, then pour in the tomato purée and maple syrup.

Remove the chicken breast from the pan, and pour the cider and balsamic mixture into the pan with the tomato purée. Blend the sauce together well and season with chile flakes, if using. Shred the cooked chicken breast with a fork and stir the pieces into the sauce.

To make the tortillas, peel and pit the avocado and slice or chop the avocado flesh into cubes. Wash, core, and cube the apple. Slice the radishes and Padrón peppers thinly. Wash, shake dry, and roughly chop the herbs. Slice the limes into eight segments. Heat the tortillas in a pan or in the oven. Fill them with your preferred combination of pulled chicken, avocado, apple, radishes, herbs, and Padrón peppers. Drizzle with lime juice before serving.

MAIN COURSES

Apple and pork make a fantastic combination. Here we cook them in the same pan for a delicious fall recipe that requires minimal attention and just a few ingredients. If you do not have any apple butter, you can caramelize the apples used in the recipe with some brown sugar, a pinch of cinnamon, and a little butter; then serve with the meat.

Pork chops with apple butter

Serves 4
Preparation 25 minutes

For the chops
4 pork chops (9oz/250g each)
salt and freshly ground
 black pepper
4 sprigs of thyme
4 sprigs of rosemary
4 large sage leaves
2 garlic cloves
2 apples (e.g. Honeycrisp,
 Cortland, McIntosh)
2 tbsp oil
3 tbsp unsalted butter
4 tsp apple butter
 (see p166)

Special equipment
meat thermometer

Season the pork chops with salt on both sides.

Wash the herbs and shake them dry. If desired, tie them together in a bundle using cooking string. Peel the garlic and crush the cloves with the flat side of a knife. Wash and core the apples, then slice each one into eight segments.

Heat the oil in a pan, add the pork chops, and fry for 1–2 minutes. Add the herbs and garlic, turn the chops, and continue frying for 1–2 minutes until they begin to take on some color. Remove the chops from the pan and set aside.

Reduce the temperature to a moderate heat and melt the butter in the pan. Add the apples and sauté for 1–2 minutes, stirring occasionally.

Spread the chops on both sides with apple butter. Make a little space in the pan and add the chops. Fry for another 2–3 minutes until the apple butter on the meat has slightly caramelized. Every so often, use a spoon to drizzle some melted butter over the chops. Season everything in the pan with salt and pepper.

Remove the chops from the pan, wrap in aluminum foil, and leave to rest for 5 minutes. To achieve the ideal cooking point, take the chops out of the pan at 155°F (68°C). Serve with the apples and a small mixed salad.

Wild boar burgers with radicchio and apple chutney

Serves 4
Preparation 35 minutes

For the burgers
1lb 5oz (600g) wild boar neck
7oz (200g) pork belly
1 tsp Worcestershire sauce
1 tbsp mustard
1 tbsp cranberry sauce
salt and freshly ground
    black pepper
3 tbsp oil

For the radicchio
5½oz (150g) radicchio
2 tbsp white balsamic
    vinegar
3 tbsp olive oil
1 tsp sugar
salt and freshly ground
    black pepper
1 small apple (e.g. Cortland)

For the sauce and burger
1 small red onion
2 pickles
2 tbsp mustard
1 tbsp cranberry sauce
about 3½oz (100g) Emmental
    or Gruyère cheese slices
4 burger buns
¼ cup apple and onion
    chutney (see p178)

Special equipment
meat grinder

Roughly chop the wild boar and pork belly before processing with a grinder. Season with Worcestershire sauce, mustard, cranberry sauce, salt, and pepper. Combine the ingredients thoroughly by hand and let them rest for 10 minutes.

Meanwhile, wash the radicchio, slice very thinly, and toss in a marinade of balsamic vinegar, olive oil, sugar, salt, and pepper. Wash the apple and grate it into the radicchio. Combine the salad ingredients thoroughly by hand and then set aside.

To make the sauce, chop the onion and pickles as finely as possible and stir them into the mustard and cranberry sauce.

Divide the meat into four equal portions and shape into burger patties. Heat the oil in a pan and fry the burgers briskly. Turn the meat and top each burger with a slice of cheese. The meat should be cooked through. Depending on how thick the burgers are, this will take 3–5 minutes on each side.

Toast the burger buns under the broiler or in a pan. Spread the bottom halves with mustard sauce and top with a burger and some radicchio. Spread each bun lid with 1 tablespoon of apple and onion chutney and place over the burger.

Wild boar is combined with spicy apple chutney, marinated radicchio, and mustard sauce to make these very special burgers. Instead of chutney, our tomato and apple jam (see p183) would also taste fantastic as the sweet component here.

Veal filet on an apple and celery root purée with a port wine sauce

Serves 4
Preparation 45 minutes

For the filet and sauce
1¾lb (800g) veal filet
8 sprigs of thyme
8 sage leaves
1 shallot
2 garlic cloves
2 tbsp butter
⅓ cup port
1 Fuji apple
1 tsp cornstarch (optional)
salt and freshly ground
    black pepper

For the purée
1¾lb (800g) celery root
3 Fuji apples
2 garlic cloves
10 tbsp butter
4¼ cups vegetable stock
4 bay leaves
4 juniper berries
½ cup milk
pinch of freshly grated
    nutmeg
Salt and freshly ground
    black pepper

Special equipment
handheld blender
meat thermometer

Slice the veal filet into 2in- (5cm-) thick medallions. Use cooking string to tie two sprigs of thyme and two sage leaves to each piece of meat. Let the meat rest.

To make the purée, peel the celery root, apples, and garlic. Core the apples, cut two of them into segments, and grate the remaining apple. Roughly chop the celery root and lightly crush the garlic cloves. Melt 2 tablespoons of butter in a pan and fry the celery root, apple segments, and garlic over a moderate heat, turning frequently. Pour in the stock. Add the bay leaves and juniper berries, cover, and simmer for 15–20 minutes until the celery root is soft.

Strain the stock through a sieve into a bowl and set aside. Add the remaining butter and the milk to the celery root, and use a hand-held blender to purée everything well. Add the grated apple and season with a pinch of nutmeg, salt, and pepper.

To make the sauce, peel and finely chop the shallot. Peel the garlic. Melt the butter in a pan and briskly fry the veal medallions for 3–4 minutes on each side. Add the garlic cloves halfway through the cooking time. Drizzle hot butter over the meat frequently. The internal temperature of medium-rare veal filets is 140°F (60°C). Remove the veal medallions from the pan, wrap in aluminum foil, and leave to rest for about 8 minutes.

Meanwhile, add the shallot to the hot pan and deglaze with the port and ½ cup of the retained vegetable stock. Wash, core, and slice the apple into segments. Add the sliced apple to the sauce. Simmer the sauce to reduce it and thicken it with cornstarch, if using. Season with salt and pepper. Serve the veal filets with the purée, apple slices, and sauce.

Apples are used in two different ways in this recipe. Apple adds a tart, fruity flavor to the mayonnaise and it works beautifully in our modified version of the classic American coleslaw. Our apple and fennel slaw has a fabulous sweet and sour, robust flavor, which works well served alongside meat or fish.

Crispy chicken with apple and fennel slaw and apple mayonnaise

Serves 4
Preparation 30 minutes

For the mayonnaise
1 medium egg yolk, at
    room temperature
1 tsp mustard
½ tsp balsamic vinegar
    or white wine vinegar
½ cup neutral-tasting oil
½ Granny Smith apple
salt and freshly ground
    black pepper

**For the apple and
    fennel slaw**
1 fennel bulb
1 Granny Smith apple
1 shallot
½ tsp anise
salt and freshly ground
    black pepper
½ bunch of chives

For the crispy chicken
1lb 2oz (500g) chicken
    breast fillet
⅓ cup cornflakes
3 medium eggs
¼ cup all-purpose flour
vegetable oil for frying

To make the mayonnaise, whisk the egg yolk, mustard, and vinegar with a balloon whisk. Pour in the oil in a thin stream, whisking constantly until you have a thick, creamy mixture. Wash and core the apple. Grate finely and stir into the mayonnaise. Season with salt and pepper.

To prepare the slaw, wash the fennel and remove the green fronds, setting these aside to use as a garnish later. Slice the fennel bulb in half and remove the base. Slice the bulb very thinly with a knife or mandoline. Wash and core the apple and slice very thinly. Peel the shallot and slice into thin rings. Add everything to a bowl, mix with three-quarters of the mayonnaise, and season to taste with anise, salt, and pepper. Wash and shake dry the chives, then chop into small rings. Mix into the salad.

Chop the chicken breast into bite-sized pieces. Pour the cornflakes into a bowl and crumble them with your fingers. Add the eggs to another bowl and whisk. Coat the chicken by tossing it first in the flour, then in the beaten egg, and finally in the cornflake crumbs. Carefully press on the coating with your fingers.

Fry the chicken nuggets in several batches in plenty of hot oil on both sides until golden brown. The oil should be between ¼ and ½in (0.5 and 1cm) deep in the pan. Remove from the pan and leave to drain on a plate lined with paper towel. If necessary, keep the nuggets warm in an oven set to 175°F (80°C) until all the pieces are cooked. Serve with the remaining apple mayonnaise and the apple and fennel slaw.

You don't need to spend ages in the kitchen to cook an unusual or special meal—as proven by our rack of lamb with apple and fennel tartare. The crunchy apple tartare goes perfectly with the tender lamb.

Rack of lamb with apple tartare and cider sauce

Serves 4
Preparation 20 minutes
Cook 20 minutes

For the lamb
2 racks of lamb
    (each with 8 ribs)
3 tbsp olive oil
2 garlic cloves
2 sprigs of rosemary
1 tbsp honey
1 tsp white balsamic vinegar
salt and freshly ground
    black pepper

For the apple tartare
2 McIntosh apples
1 fennel bulb
1 carrot
zest and juice of 1
    organic lime
1 tsp olive oil
salt and freshly ground
    black pepper

For the cider sauce
½ cup hard cider
¾ cup heavy cream
salt and freshly ground
    black pepper

Preheat the oven to 250°F (120°C). Briskly fry the racks of lamb in a pan with 1 tablespoon of olive oil, first on the fatty sides, then the other sides for about 2 minutes each. Remove from the pan and set the pan aside for making the sauce later. Peel and finely slice the garlic. Wash and shake dry the rosemary. Stir together the remaining olive oil, garlic, honey, and vinegar to make a marinade. Season with salt and pepper.

Brush the lamb with the marinade, transfer to an ovenproof dish, and top each rack with a sprig of rosemary. Cook the lamb in the oven on the middle shelf for 15–20 minutes, depending on the size of the racks.

Meanwhile, make the apple tartare. Wash and dry the apples and fennel bulb. Halve the fennel and set one half aside for the sauce and remove any fronds, to use as a garnish later. Peel the carrot. Finely chop the apples, carrot, and fennel into equal-sized pieces. Add these to a bowl and mix. Add the lime juice, zest, and oil, and season the tartare with salt and pepper.

To make the sauce, thinly slice the remaining half of fennel and fry these strips in the pan used for the meat. After about 2 minutes, deglaze the pan with cider and add the heavy cream. Simmer the sauce for 5 minutes.

Remove the meat from the oven and add the juices to the sauce. Allow the racks of lamb to rest for 5 minutes. Season the sauce to taste with salt and pepper. Serve the meat with the tartare, sauce, and, if desired, the fennel fronds.

Apple meets chicken to create a delicious dish that is incredibly easy to prepare. The salsa gives these kebabs a fruity flavor. We recommend rice or couscous as a side dish.

Chicken kebabs with apple salsa

Serves 4
Preparation 25 minutes
Cook 20 minutes

For the marinade
1 tsp tomato paste
3 tbsp white balsamic
    vinegar
3 tbsp oil
1 tsp sweet ground paprika
1 tsp soy sauce
1½ tsp honey
1 garlic clove
salt and freshly ground
    black pepper

For the kebabs
1lb 2oz (500g) chicken
    breast fillet
5½oz (150g) onions
5½oz (150g) smoked
    pancetta or bacon
oil for frying
shoots, such as pea or mung
    bean, to garnish (optional)

For the salsa
2 red bell peppers
1 Granny Smith apple
1–2 tsp honey
1 tbsp vinegar
1 tbsp oil
lemon juice for drizzling

Special equipment
handheld blender

To make the marinade, combine the tomato paste, balsamic vinegar, oil, paprika, soy sauce, and honey in a small bowl. Peel and crush the garlic, and add to the marinade with some salt and pepper.

Chop the chicken breast into roughly ³/₄in (2cm) pieces. Peel the onion and slice into wedges. Slice the bacon or pancetta. Slide alternate pieces of chicken, bacon, and onion onto the skewers. Brush the kebabs all over with the marinade.

Meanwhile, preheat the oven to 400°F (200°C). Halve and seed the peppers. Place them on a baking sheet lined with parchment paper and roast in the oven on the top shelf for about 20 minutes until the skins are black and blistered. Plunge the peppers briefly in ice-cold water and remove the skins with a small knife.

Roughly chop the flesh. Wash, core, and halve the apple. Chop one half into large pieces and use a handheld blender to purée these with the pepper, 2 tablespoons of water, honey, vinegar, and oil. Season with salt and pepper. Finely cube the other half of the apple, drizzle with lemon juice, and set aside.

Heat the oil in a large pan. Fry the skewers on all sides over a moderate heat. Brush repeatedly with the marinade while cooking.

Arrange the skewers on plates with the salsa, and garnish with the cubed apple and some fresh shoots, if using.

Festive menus of delicious food are an essential part of Christmas for us. One classic dish is crispy roast duck, which we stuff with apples, dates, and chestnuts. Potato dumplings and apple with red cabbage (see p64) make great side dishes.

Roast duck with a date, apple, and chestnut stuffing

Serves 4
Preparation 25 minutes
Cook 1½–2 hours

For the duck
1 free-range duck,
    about 5lb (2.25kg),
    with giblets
3 apples (e.g. Honeycrisp,
    Cortland, or McIntosh)
7oz (200g) dried dates
7oz (200g) cooked chestnuts
1 tsp anise
salt and freshly ground
    black pepper
2 red onions
5 star anise
2 dried chiles (e.g. árbol)
1 tsp cardamom pods
1 tsp ground allspice
1 cup chicken stock

For the caramelized apples
1 apple
1 tbsp oil
2 tbsp granulated sugar
¼ cup pastis or
    apple juice

For the sauce
3 shallots
1 tbsp oil
1 tsp confectioner's sugar
⅔ cup port
salt and freshly ground
    black pepper
1 tsp cornstarch (optional)

Preheat the oven to 350°F (180°C). Use tweezers to remove any remaining plumage from the duck. Remove the parson's nose and the neck if necessary. Set aside the tail, neck, and giblets.

To make the stuffing, wash, quarter, and core the apples. Cube the dates, chestnuts, and four of the apple quarters, and mix. Season with anise, salt, and pepper. Put three-quarters of the stuffing inside the duck. Close the bottom of the duck with a toothpick. Tie the legs together with cooking string.

Quarter the onions and scatter these with the remaining apples in a roasting pan. Add the remaining stuffing and season with star anise, chiles, cardamom, and allspice. Place the duck on top and transfer into the oven. Fill an ovenproof or casserole dish with 2 cups of boiling hot water and place this at the bottom of the oven. Roast the duck in the oven on the bottom shelf for 1½–2 hours. After 20 minutes, pour over some chicken stock, and repeat this at regular intervals. Insert a skewer into the area at the top

of the leg where it meets the body. If the juices run clear, the duck is cooked.

In the meantime, slice the apple thinly. Heat the oil in a pan and fry the sliced apple briskly. After 30 seconds, sprinkle over the granulated sugar and pour in the pastis or apple juice. If you're using the pastis, flambé by carefully igniting it with kitchen matches or a stove lighter.

To make the sauce, finely chop the shallots. Remove the roast duck from the oven and strain the juices through a sieve. Heat the oil in a pan and sauté the shallots until translucent. Add the confectioner's sugar, the giblets, the parson's nose, and the neck, and continue frying. Deglaze with port and add the juices retained from the meat. Bring to a boil. If you're using cornstarch to thicken, stir ¼ cup of the sauce into some cornstarch in a bowl, return this mixture to the sauce, and bring to a boil briefly, stirring constantly. Remove the giblets, parson's nose, and neck, then season the sauce with salt and pepper. Serve the duck with the sliced apple and sauce.

Oven-roasted red cabbage is a fantastic alternative to the traditional braised recipe. Being cooked in the oven, the vegetable retains some bite and gets a more intense, roasted flavour. This dish is ideal served with apple segments, succulent roast beef, and crispy fried onions.

Roast beef with fried onions and oven-baked apple and red cabbage

Serves 4
Preparation 15 minutes
Cook 65 minutes

For the roast beef
1¾lb (800g) beef sirloin
oil for frying

For the red cabbage
about 14oz (400g)
    red cabbage
2 firm apples (e.g. Fuji,
    Pink Lady, Jonagold)
¼ cup olive oil, plus extra
    for greasing and drizzling
2 tbsp cider vinegar
2 tsp honey
juice of ½ lemon
salt and freshly ground
    black pepper

For the onions
1 onion
1 cup oil
3 tbsp all-purpose flour
pinch of salt

Special equipment
meat thermometer

Allow the beef to come to room temperature. Preheat the oven to 350°F (180°C). Remove the external leaves from the cabbage, slice it in half, and remove the stalk. Cut the cabbage into roughly ¹/₂in- (1cm-) thick slices. Wash and core the apples then cut into wedges or slices.

Make a marinade by combining the oil, vinegar, honey, lemon juice, salt, and pepper. Grease a baking tray with olive oil, add the sliced red cabbage, and drizzle with the marinade. Bake in the oven on the middle shelf for 25 minutes, then add the sliced apple, drizzle with a little olive oil, and continue cooking for another 15 minutes.

Fry the sirloin to seal it, first on the fatty side, then on the other sides. Place it on the red cabbage with the fat facing upward and cook for about 25 minutes, or until it has reached an internal core temperature of 127°F (53°C) for rare beef. Cook for longer if you prefer your meat medium-rare, medium, or well done. Take the meat out of the oven, wrap in aluminum foil, and leave to rest for about 5 minutes.

Meanwhile, prepare the fried onions. Peel the onion and slice into rings. Heat the oil in a small pan. Put the flour in a deep dish with a pinch of salt and toss the onion in this mixture. Fry the onion in the oil and leave to drain on paper towel.

Slice the roast beef thinly against the grain and season with salt and pepper. Serve with the baked red cabbage, apples, and onion rings.

This quiche is given a robust, spicy flavor thanks to the addition of Spanish chorizo. The chorizo has a slight kick, and its spiciness goes beautifully with the sweet and tangy flavor of apples.

Apple and Swiss chard quiche with chorizo

Makes 1 quiche, 11in (28cm) diameter
Preparation 30 minutes
Rest 1 hour
Cook 40 minutes

For the pastry
9 tbsp cold butter
1¼ cups white spelt flour
½ tsp salt
1 medium egg

For the filling
1 leek
2 apples
5½oz (150g) medium-
 hot chorizo
¼ cup plus 1 tsp hazelnuts
3½oz (100g) baby
 Swiss chard
¾ cup sour cream
2 medium eggs
2oz (60g) Parmesan cheese,
 grated
salt and freshly ground
 black pepper

Special equipment
loose-bottomed 11in (28cm)
 fluted tart pan

Cube the butter for the pastry. Mix the flour and salt, add the butter, 1 egg, and 3–4 tablespoons of ice-cold water, and mix together quickly so the ingredients combine. Shape the pastry into a ball, wrap it in plastic wrap, and let it rest in the fridge for 1 hour. Preheat the oven to 400°F (200°C).

Wash the leek and apples. Slice the leek into rings, and core and slice the apples. Remove the skin from the chorizo and slice into rounds. Roughly chop the hazelnuts. Wash the baby Swiss chard and leave to drain. Set aside a couple of leaves for garnish (optional). Whisk together the sour cream, 2 eggs, and Parmesan cheese, season with salt and pepper, and set aside.

Briefly fry the chorizo, leek, and apples in a pan over a high heat.

Reduce the temperature, and add the nuts and Swiss chard. Stir together until the Swiss chard is wilting slightly. Season with salt and pepper.

Roll out the pastry on a lightly floured work surface until it is slightly larger than the tart pan. Lift the pastry into the pan, press the edges with your fingers, and prick the base all over with a fork.

Spread half of the chorizo and apple filling over the base, pour in the egg mixture, and scatter the remaining filling ingredients on top. Bake in the oven on the middle shelf for 35–40 minutes until golden and leave to cool slightly. Garnish with Swiss chard leaves, if using, and serve lukewarm. This goes beautifully with a mixed lettuce salad.

The inspiration for our stuffed, oven-baked trout came from our travels in Portugal. Portuguese cooking is renowned for its simple style, with regional ingredients being used to create unpretentious but delicious recipes. For our trout, we also focused on just a few high-quality ingredients, most of which can be sourced locally.

Oven-baked trout with a cream cheese and apple filling

Serves 4
Preparation 20 minutes
Cook 25 minutes

For the trout
4 trout, about 9oz (250g)
    each, scaled, gutted, and
    ready to cook
salt and freshly ground
    black pepper
1 bunch of parsley
14oz (400g) full-fat
    cream cheese
2 apples (e.g. McIntosh,
    Pink Lady, Jonagold)
2 organic lemons

Preheat the oven to 400°F (200°C). Rinse the trout inside and out with cold water and pat dry with paper towel. Season the inside cavity of the trout with salt and pepper. Wash, shake dry, and chop the parsley. Season the cream cheese with salt and pepper and fold in the parsley. Cut the apples and lemons into medium-sized slices.

Cut four sheets of baking paper 20 x 16in (about 50 x 40cm). Place the trout on the sheets, and fill each cavity with three or four slices of apple and lemon and the cream cheese. Fold the baking paper loosely over the trout to make little parcels and tie up the ends with cooking string, making sure it is not too close to the fish. Place the parcels on a baking tray.

Cook the trout in the oven on the middle shelf for about 25 minutes. Remove the fish from the oven and test to see if it is done by pulling out the dorsal (top) fin on the largest fish. If the flesh on the bones is cooked, the rest of the fish will be ready. If not, continue cooking for 5–10 minutes. Baked potatoes and grilled vegetables go beautifully with this dish.

These clams cooked in cider bring a Mediterranean feel to the table. Remember that when preparing clams and other shellfish, you should discard any that have a cracked or broken shell, or if the shells are open and do not close when tapped. Also discard any clams that fail to open when cooked.

Clams in cider with linguine

Serves 4
Preparation 30 minutes

For the clams
2¼lb (1kg) clams
2 onions
2 garlic cloves
7oz (200g) carrots
9oz (250g) cherry tomatoes
7oz (200g) celery
1 bunch of parsley
3 tbsp olive oil
1 tsp anise
1 tbsp tomato paste
11fl oz (330ml) hard cider
14oz (400g) linguine
    or spaghetti
salt and freshly ground
    black pepper
1 tsp chile flakes
olive oil for drizzling

Carefully clean the clams. Discard any that are open or damaged, wash the closed clams thoroughly several times in water, and leave to drain.

Peel and roughly chop the onions. Peel the garlic and carrots, and cut the carrots into small cubes. Wash the tomatoes and celery, removing any long, stringy fibers from the celery with a small knife. Slice the celery into thin rings and chop finely. Wash, shake dry, and chop the parsley.

Heat the oil in a large pan. Add the onions, carrots, garlic cloves, and celery, and sauté over a moderate heat until translucent. Add the clams, tomatoes, anise, half the parsley, and the tomato paste. Fry briefly, and then pour in the cider. Bring to a boil, cover, and simmer for about 8–10 minutes until the clams have opened. Discard any clams that have failed to open.

Meanwhile, cook the linguine according to the instructions on the packet until it is al dente. Drain and add the linguine to the clams. Season with salt, pepper, parsley, and chile flakes, and mix everything together well.

Serve on deep plates and drizzle with olive oil before serving.

Hasselback potatoes are a favorite side dish in our house. For a variation on this theme, try our Hasselback apples with bacon, Parmesan cheese, and sage. We serve these with baked sea bass, a hazelnut crumble, and a delicious white wine sauce.

Baked sea bass with Hasselback apples, hazelnut crumble, and white wine sauce

Serves 4
Preparation 25 minutes
Cook 1 hour

For the apples and potatoes
2 Fuji apples
8 medium red potatoes
2–3 tbsp olive oil
salt and freshly ground
   black pepper
3½oz (100g) bacon or
   pancetta
2¾oz (80g) Parmesan cheese
1 bunch of sage

For the crumble
2 tbsp butter
½ cup plus 3 tbsp
   breadcrumbs
¾oz (about 14 nuts)
   hazelnuts
salt and freshly ground
   black pepper

For the sea bass and sauce
4 sea bass fillets, about 7oz
   (200g) each, skin on
¼ cup plus 1 tbsp all-purpose
   flour
2–3 tbsp oil
1 garlic clove
¼ cup heavy cream
3½ tbsp white wine

Special equipment
handheld blender

Preheat the oven to 400°F (200°C). Wash the apples and potatoes. Halve the apples and slice them Hasselback style—slice thinly (about $^1/_{16}$in/2mm wide) from the skin side down, but do not cut all the way through (see Tip, below right). Slice the potatoes in a similar Hasselback style. Brush the potatoes with oil and season with salt. Slice the bacon and Parmesan as thinly as possible. Wash and shake dry the sage, setting aside two leaves for the sauce. Cut any large leaves in half. Insert bacon, sage, and Parmesan alternately into the cuts in the potatoes and apples.

Place the potatoes on a baking sheet lined with parchment paper. Bake in the oven on the middle shelf for 20 minutes. Remove them briefly, brush with oil, and add the apples to the baking sheet. Return to the oven for a further 30–40 minutes until the apples are soft and the potatoes are cooked.

Meanwhile, to make the crumble topping, melt the butter in a pan, add the breadcrumbs, and brown these gently over a moderate heat, stirring constantly. Roughly chop the hazelnuts and add them to the breadcrumbs. Season with salt and pepper and set aside.

Wash the fish, pat it dry, and make two small incisions on the skin side with a sharp knife. Toss the fillets in flour. Heat the oil in a pan and fry the fillets skin-side down for 2–3 minutes. Turn them and fry for another 30 seconds. Remove the fish from the pan and keep warm in the oven at 170°F (75°C).

Peel the garlic for the sauce. Add the reserved sage leaves and garlic to the hot pan, pour in the heavy cream and white wine, and simmer for 1 minute. Transfer the sauce to a blender beaker and briefly froth using a handheld blender. Serve the fish with the apples, potatoes, and sauce, and garnish with hazelnut crumble.

Tip: rest the potato or apple on a large serving spoon before making the incisions—cutting on a spoon stops you from slicing all the way through.

Sweet, caramelized apple slices add a special touch to this recipe. An herby crumble topping with creamy sauce and blueberries provides the perfect garnish for a delicious meal that looks as good as it tastes.

Salmon fillets with caramelized apple and a blueberry and herb topping

Serves 4
Preparation 30 minutes

For the salmon fillet
1¾lb (800g) salmon fillet,
  skin on
1–2 tbsp oil

For the herb crumble
1 bunch of parsley
1 bunch of chives
1 sprig of sage
2 tbsp butter
½ cup plus 3 tbsp
  breadcrumbs
salt and freshly ground
  black pepper

For the apple
1 apple (e.g. Pink Lady,
  McIntosh, Jonagold)
2 tbsp confectioner's sugar

For the sauces
½ garlic clove
¼ cup heavy cream
3½ tbsp sour cream
7oz (200g) blueberries

Special equipment
handheld blender

Rinse the salmon fillet, pat it dry, and divide into four pieces.

For the crumble, wash and shake dry the parsley, chives, and sage. Pick the sage leaves off the stalk and finely chop all the herbs. Melt the butter in a pan and fry the breadcrumbs over a moderate heat until golden. Mix with the herbs and season with salt and pepper.

Wash the apple, rub it dry, and slice into thin rings. Lightly dust these on both sides with confectioner's sugar. Heat the apple rings on both sides in a pan over a moderate heat to caramelize them.

Peel the garlic for the cream sauce. Use a handheld blender to purée it with the heavy cream and sour cream until the mixture is smooth and frothy. Season with salt and pepper.

To make the blueberry sauce, put half the blueberries in a small pan with 2 tablespoons of water and bring briefly to a boil. Crush the berries with a fork or spatula.

Heat the oil in a pan and fry the salmon fillets skin-side down for 4–6 minutes. The cooking time will depend on the thickness of the fish. Then turn the fillets over and fry for 30 seconds.

Arrange the fish on plates with the caramelized apple slices. Sprinkle with the herb crumble. Add small dollops of the blueberry and cream sauces, and garnish with the remaining blueberries.

Things are heating up! Som tam salad is originally from Laos, and it brings a little spice to the table. The dish is traditionally made using green papaya, which is mashed with the other ingredients in a pestle and mortar. For our recipe, we have replaced the papaya with crunchy green apples. The combination of fruity apple, sour lime, spicy chile, and salty fish sauce produces a real explosion of flavors on the palate.

Thai som tam salad with green apples

Serves 4
Preparation 40 minutes

For the dressing
1 organic lime, plus extra
    for garnish
2 tbsp tamarind paste
3 tbsp fish sauce
3 tbsp brown sugar

For the salad
2¾oz (80g) dried shrimp
    (available from Asian
    stores)
4 Granny Smith apples
2–3 red bird's eye (Thai)
    chiles (depending on
    how spicy you want the
    dish to be)
16 cherry tomatoes
3½oz (100g) sugar snap peas
4 garlic cloves
½ cup roasted peanuts
1 cup fresh cilantro, chopped
1 sprig of Thai basil

For the dressing, wash the lime, slice it in half, and squeeze the juice. Set aside the squeezed halves for later. Combine the juice with 2 tablespoons of water, the tamarind paste, fish sauce, and sugar, and stir well.

Soak the dried shrimp in lukewarm water. Wash and core the apples, and cut them into thin, fine julienne strips. Wash and dry the chiles and tomatoes. Remove the stems from the chiles. Wash the sugar snap peas and use a sharp knife to remove the thin string that runs down the side. Peel the garlic cloves and roughly chop the peanuts.

Drain the shrimp and chop roughly. Add the shrimp to a pestle and mortar and crush them along with the lime halves you set aside earlier, the garlic,

and the chiles. Add the sugar snap peas and cherry tomatoes, and crush these slightly. Add about a third of the apple and continue crushing everything carefully. Transfer the crushed ingredients to a larger bowl, removing the lime halves. Stir in the remaining apples, peanuts, and dressing. Finally, mash everything carefully once again and mix well to combine. Wash, shake dry, and roughly chop the cilantro and Thai basil, and mix these into the salad. Serve with slices of lime.

Som tam tastes wonderful on its own or with some steamed jasmine rice.

Nothing tastes better than homemade pasta. Flo and I love experimenting with different pasta doughs and fillings, particularly for special occasions. Homemade tortellini is one of our absolute favorites. Making these stuffed parcels yourself looks more complicated than it is. You just need a couple of tries and you will be filling and folding like a professional.

Beet tortellini with an apple and Roquefort filling

Serves 4
Preparation 1–1½ hours

For the tortellini
2⅓ cups 00 grade pasta flour, plus a little extra for working, or 1 cup all-purpose flour and ¾ cup durum wheat semolina
1 tsp salt
½ cup beet juice
1 medium egg
1 tbsp oil

For the filling
3½oz (100g) Roquefort cheese
3½oz (100g) full-fat cream cheese
½ medium apple (e.g. Jonagold, Pink Lady, Gala)

For the sauce
1 garlic clove
1 sprig of thyme
1 sprig of rosemary
2 tbsp olive oil
½ cup dry white wine
¾ cup heavy cream
salt and freshly ground black pepper

To serve
Parmesan cheese, grated
¼ apple, grated
zest of ½ organic lemon
7oz (200g) Brussels sprouts (optional)

To make the tortellini, first combine the flour and salt. Add the beet juice, egg, and oil, and work with your hands for 5–10 minutes until you have an elastic dough. If it is too sticky, add some more flour. Wrap in plastic wrap and let it rest for at least 30 minutes.

To make the filling, stir the Roquefort and cream cheese together until smooth. Wash, quarter, core, and finely grate the apple. Stir this into the Roquefort and cream cheese mixture. Caution: the mixture should not be too liquid. If your apple is on the larger size, use a little less of it. Put the filling into the fridge to chill.

Roll out the pasta dough in sections on a lightly floured surface so it is $^1/_{16}$–$^1/_8$in (2–3mm) thick. Rewrap any dough you are not currently using in plastic wrap to stop it drying out. Use a cutter to cut out circles 3in (8cm) in diameter. Put 1 teaspoon of the filling in the center of each circle. Moisten the edges with a little water and fold the dough over to make a semicircle. Squeeze the edges together firmly. Position the

parcel so its thickest part rests on your index finger and wrap the ends around your finger. If necessary, moisten the ends slightly to bind them together. Place each parcel on a lightly floured surface until all the tortellini have been shaped. Bring a large pan of salted water to a boil.

Finely chop the garlic to make the sauce. Wash and shake dry the herbs. Add oil to a pan and sauté the garlic over a moderate heat until translucent. Deglaze the pan with wine and, after about 1 minute, add the cream and herbs. Simmer for 5 minutes, and then season with salt and pepper. Remove the herbs.

Add the tortellini to the boiling water in batches. Cook for 1–2 minutes. Use a slotted spoon to remove them and serve with the sauce, Parmesan, grated apple, and lemon zest. Blanch the Brussels sprouts, if using, and serve with those too.

Squash and apple strudel

Serves 8–10
Preparation 40 minutes
Cook 45 minutes

For the filling
14oz (400g) butternut
    squash, unpeeled
3 small apples (e.g. Cortland,
    Honeycrisp, Fuji)
1 onion
¼oz (10g) ginger
1 sprig of rosemary
½ cup plus 1 tbsp cooked
    chestnuts
3½oz (100g) spinach
1 medium egg
½ cup plus 1 tbsp (3½fl oz)
    full-fat crème fraîche
2 tbsp butter
salt and freshly ground
    black pepper
pinch of freshly grated
    nutmeg
oil for brushing

For the yogurt dip
2 sprigs of parsley
½ cup full-fat yogurt
1 tsp white balsamic vinegar
1 tsp olive oil
pinch of sugar
1 tsp lemon juice

For the strudel
1 packet store-bought filo
    pastry or homemade
    strudel pastry (see p99)

Special equipment
Pastry cloth or large kitchen
    towel

Wash the squash and apples, remove the core and seeds, and cut into ¹/₂in (1cm) cubes. Peel and finely chop the onion and ginger. Wash and shake dry the rosemary and finely chop the needles. Roughly chop the chestnuts. Wash and drain the spinach, and shred roughly. Mix the egg and crème fraîche together in a bowl.

Melt the butter in a pan and fry the onions and squash for about 5 minutes. Add the rosemary, chestnuts, and ginger, and continue frying briefly. Add the spinach and continue cooking until the leaves have wilted. Transfer everything into a bowl and leave to cool. Once the filling is lukewarm, add the apples and crème fraîche mixture and stir well. Season with salt, pepper, and a pinch of nutmeg.

Wash the parsley for the yogurt dip, shake it dry, and chop finely. Mix this with the other dip ingredients in a small bowl and refrigerate. Preheat the oven to 400°F (200°C).

If you are using homemade strudel pastry, roll it out and stretch it on a kitchen towel or pastry cloth (see p99), then brush with oil. If you are using ready-made filo pastry, place one sheet on a damp cloth and brush with oil. Place a second sheet on top and brush with oil. Add another two sheets of pastry brushed with oil. Spread the filling out over the lower third of the pastry, leaving a space of about 1¹/₂–2in (4–5cm) around the edge. Fold the sides over the filling and roll up the strudel using the cloth to help you.

Place the strudel, seam facing down, on a baking sheet lined with baking paper and brush again with oil. Bake in the oven on the middle shelf for about 45 minutes until crisp and brown. Brush with oil again after about 30 minutes. Serve with the yogurt dip.

Apple, squash, and chestnuts—this strudel contains the most delicious fruit and vegetables that fall has to offer. Of course, it tastes best with homemade pastry. You'll find a recipe and instructions for this on pp98–99, but if you're short of time, you can also use store-bought filo pastry.

Beet and apple risotto brings a touch of color to the table as well as being incredibly tasty. This root vegetable's earthy flavor goes beautifully with sweet and tangy apples. A delicate crunch is introduced with a topping of toasted sliced almonds.

Beet and apple risotto with toasted sliced almonds

Serves 4
Preparation 30 minutes

For the risotto
2 red onions
1lb 2oz (500g) cooked beets
2 apples (e.g. Fuji, McIntosh)
3½oz (100g) Parmesan
   cheese
1 sprig of thyme
3 tbsp olive oil
14oz (400g) risotto rice
2 cups hard cider
3 cups vegetable stock
¼ cup sliced almonds
½ tsp ground cinnamon
2 tsp granulated sugar
salt and freshly ground
   black pepper
8 apple chips (see p170)

Peel and finely chop the onions, and cut the beets into cubes. Wash, core, and cube the apples. Grate the Parmesan. Wash and shake dry the thyme, and then strip off the leaves.

Heat the oil in a pan and sauté the onions until translucent. Add the rice and continue frying for about 3 minutes. Deglaze the pan with a dash of cider. Then simmer over a low heat, stirring regularly, until the rice has absorbed the liquid. Gradually add small quantities of stock and cider, stirring occasionally. Only add the next batch of liquid once the rice has absorbed the liquid in the pan. The risotto is ready when it has a creamy consistency and the rice is cooked al dente (about 20 minutes). Add the beets and apples shortly before the end of the cooking time and heat them through for about 2 minutes.

Meanwhile, toast the sliced almonds with the cinnamon and sugar in a dry pan until golden brown.

Stir 2¾oz (80g) grated Parmesan into the risotto and season with salt and pepper. Add the thyme leaves. Garnish with sliced almonds, the remaining Parmesan, and a couple of the apple chips for each serving.

This recipe is perfect if you haven't got much time to make dinner: baked feta with apples, tomatoes, and onions. It's one of our favorite weekday meals. And with good reason because you can have it in the oven in 5 minutes, and about 20 minutes later, supper is on the table. Incredibly simple and packed with flavor!

Oven-baked feta

Serves 4
Preparation 10 minutes
Cook 20 minutes

4–5 tbsp olive oil, plus extra
    for drizzling
juice of ½ lemon
1 tsp honey
salt and freshly ground
    black pepper
3 red onions
4 firm apples
    (e.g. Fuji, Jonagold,
    Northern Spy)
9oz (250g) cherry tomatoes
    on the vine
4 sprigs of parsley
14oz (400g) feta cheese

Put the oil, lemon juice, and honey in a bowl, and stir to combine. Season with salt and pepper.

Preheat the oven to 400°F (200°C). Peel the onions and cut into halves or quarters, depending on their size. Wash the apples and tomatoes. Wash, shake dry, and roughly chop the parsley.

Drain the feta and put it into an ovenproof dish. Cut about half the apples into slices and spread these over the feta. Add the remaining apples to the dish, either as they are or in wedges, depending on their size. Scatter the tomatoes and onions around the dish.

Pour the lemon and oil marinade over the feta and vegetables and scatter with parsley. Bake in the oven on the middle shelf for 20 minutes. Drizzle with olive oil and serve with bread or salad.

We love sauntering through a local market on a Saturday, seeking inspiration from whatever seasonal produce is available. In fall, we like to use apple, squash, and beets to make a shortcrust (pie crust) galette. A parsley and feta garnish transforms this simple pastry into a delicious fall dish.

Apple and squash galette with beets and feta

Serves 8
Preparation 30 minutes
Rest 1 hour
Cook 45 minutes

For the pastry
11 tbsp cold butter
3 cups white spelt flour
1 tsp salt
¼ cup milk, plus extra
   for brushing

For the filling
1 garlic clove
7fl oz (200ml) sour cream
1 tbsp lemon juice
3 sprigs of thyme
salt and freshly ground
   black pepper

For the topping
1–2 apples (e.g. Pink Lady,
   Fuji), about 10oz (300g)
about 7oz (200g) Hokkaido
   (red kuri) squash,
   unpeeled
1 large red onion
7oz (200g) cooked beets
3½oz (100g) feta
2 tsp parsley

To make the shortcrust pastry, first cut the butter into cubes. Mix the flour and salt. Add the butter and milk, and gradually pour in ½ cup of ice-cold water, working everything together swiftly. It does not matter if you can still see small flecks of butter in the pastry—this will ensure the galette has a beautifully flaky texture. Shape the pastry into a flat slab, wrap it in plastic wrap, and let it rest in the fridge for about 1 hour. Preheat the oven to 400°F (200°C).

To make the filling, peel and crush the garlic. Combine the sour cream, garlic, and lemon juice. Wash and shake dry the thyme, strip the leaves, and add to the mixture. Season with salt and pepper.

Wash the apples and squash, remove the core and seeds, and slice into thin segments. Peel the onion and slice into rings. Slice the beets. Wash, shake dry, and chop the parsley. Finely crumble the feta with your fingers and mix with the parsley. Put the mixture in the fridge.

Roll out the pastry on a lightly floured work surface to create a circular disk ⅛in (3–4mm) thick. Place the disk on a baking sheet lined with parchment paper. Spread the filling mixture over the pastry, leaving a gap of about 2in (5cm) around the edge.

Top with alternate slices of apple, squash, onion, and beets. Fold the edges of the pastry over the topping and brush with a little milk. Bake the galette in the oven on the middle shelf for 40–45 minutes until golden. Scatter over the crumbled feta and serve warm.

Dal is India's national dish and one of our favorite recipes, especially in fall and winter. Dal is a traditional dish made from legumes, usually lentils. It's quick and easy to make and really filling thanks to the high fiber content. A grated apple adds a fruity element to the dish.

Red lentil dal with grated apple

Serves 4
Preparation 30 minutes

2 red onions
3 garlic cloves
¾oz (20g) ginger
3 carrots
1¾ cup plus 2 tbsp red lentils
2½ tbsp coconut oil
1½ tsp ground cumin
1½ tbsp curry powder
5½oz (150g) grated tart
   apple (e.g. Granny
   Smith, Cortland)
2½ cups coconut milk
10oz (300g) canned
   chopped tomatoes
2½oz (75g) baby spinach
juice of 1 lime
salt and freshly ground
   black pepper
¼ cup full-fat yogurt
2 tbsp unsweetened
   shredded coconut
apple slices and spinach
   leaves to garnish
   (optional)

Peel and finely chop the onions, garlic, ginger, and carrots. Rinse the lentils and leave to drain.

Melt the coconut oil in a pan and sauté the chopped onion over a moderate heat. Add the garlic, ginger, carrots, cumin, and curry powder, and continue frying for 3–4 minutes, stirring constantly. Stir in the lentils and grated apple. Add 2 cups of water, the coconut milk, and tomatoes. Cover and simmer for 15 minutes over a moderate heat.

Wash the spinach and dry it in a salad spinner. Mix the spinach leaves into the dal and let it stand for about 5 minutes. Adjust the seasoning with lime juice, salt, and pepper.

Serve the dal in small bowls, topped with yogurt and coconut. Garnish with apple slices and spinach leaves, if using.

BAKING
AND CAKES

Cheesecake with an apple crumble topping

Makes 1 cheesecake, 9½ or 10¼in (24 or 26cm) diameter
Preparation 35 minutes
Cook 1 hour 20 minutes

For the crumble topping
3 tbsp cold butter
⅔ cup all-purpose flour
3 tbsp granulated sugar
½ tsp ground cinnamon
pinch of salt

For the base
11 graham crackers
5 tbsp butter, plus extra
    for greasing
pinch of salt

For the apple topping
4 medium apples (e.g.
    Jonagold, Northern Spy)
juice of ½ lemon
2 tbsp brown sugar
1 tsp ground cinnamon
2–3 tbsp cornstarch

For the filling
1¾lb (800g) full-fat
    cream cheese
1 cup granulated sugar
¼ cup cornstarch
1 tsp vanilla extract
zest and juice of ½ lemon
7fl oz (200ml) sour cream
3 medium eggs

Special equipment
9½ or 10¼in (24 or 26cm)
    springform pan
electric hand whisk

About 1 hour before you start cooking, take all the chilled ingredients (except the butter for the crumble) out of the fridge and allow them to come to room temperature.

Add all the ingredients for the crumble to a bowl and rub them together with your fingers until you have a crumbly consistency. Transfer to the fridge.

Preheat the oven to 350°F (180°C). Line the base of a springform pan with parchment paper and grease the sides.

Finely grind the graham crackers. Melt the butter in a small pan over a moderate heat and pour it over the graham-cracker crumbs. Add the salt. Stir everything together until well mixed. Spread the graham-cracker mixture over the base of the pan and press down firmly with a spoon. Bake in a preheated oven on the middle shelf for 10 minutes. Remove from the oven and put aside to cool.

Meanwhile, prepare the apple topping. Peel, core, and cube the apples. Add the apple to a pan

with the lemon juice, brown sugar, cinnamon, and 2 cups of water, bring to a boil, and simmer for 4–5 minutes over a moderate heat. Stir in the cornstarch and bring to a boil briefly, stirring constantly. Remove from the stove. Reduce the temperature of the oven to 300°F (150°C).

To make the filling, beat the cream cheese and sugar together using an electric hand whisk on the lowest setting. Stir in the cornstarch, vanilla extract, lemon zest and juice, and sour cream. Beat the eggs in a small bowl and fold them into the cream cheese mixture in two stages. Spread the filling over the graham-cracker base and smooth it out. Scatter the apples on top, followed by the crumble topping.

Bake in the oven on the middle shelf for 1 hour 10 minutes. Remove, leave to cool slightly, and release from the pan. Allow the cheesecake to cool completely before putting it in the fridge. Let the flavors develop in the fridge for a couple of hours for the best taste.

Our tarte tatin is a quick and easy version of this classic French dish. We love the caramel aroma that wafts through our home while this is baking, enhancing the mouthwatering anticipation of the finished dish.

Tarte tatin

**Makes 1 tart, 10¼ or 11in (26 or 28cm) diameter
Preparation 20 minutes
Cook 30 minutes**

juice of ½ lemon
4–5 medium sweet and
    tangy apples (e.g. Idared,
    Fuji, Northern Spy)
½ cup sugar
¼ cup Calvados (apple
    brandy)
2 tbsp butter
pinch of salt
9oz (250g) store-bought puff
    pastry (chilled)

Special equipment
10¼ or 11in (26 or 28cm)
    round tart pan

Fill a large bowl with water and add the lemon juice. Peel and core the apples, then cut them into segments about ¹/₂in (1cm) thick. Put them in the bowl of water to prevent them going brown. Preheat the oven to 350°F (180°C).

Put the sugar in a pan with 3 tablespoons of water and cook over a moderate heat until the sugar has melted and caramelized to a golden brown. Do not stir during this process. Pour in the Calvados and simmer to reduce the liquid a little while stirring. Remove from the stove. Cut the butter into pieces. Add the salt and butter pieces to the pan and stir everything until you have a thick caramel mixture. Transfer into a tart pan or ovenproof dish.

Remove the slices of apple from the water and drain thoroughly. Arrange in a spiral pattern on top of the caramel mixture.

Roll out the puff pastry, cut it into a disc that is slightly larger than the pan, and cover the apples with the pastry. Press down the edges with your fingers and prick small holes in the pastry with a fork. Bake in a preheated oven on the middle shelf for 25–30 minutes until the puff pastry is golden.

Remove from the oven, leave to cool slightly, and loosen the edges with a small knife. Carefully turn out the tart using a plate to help you. Ideally, use a plate with a slight lip to prevent the hot caramel sauce running over the sides.

The tart is best served lukewarm, perhaps with some crème fraîche or ice cream.

Of all the amazing treats baked by Madeleine's granny, nothing beats her homemade apple strudel. We always knew our book would include this old family recipe. A delicate, buttery, flaky pastry envelops a delicious filling of grated apples, raisins, sugar, and cinnamon. Every mouthful brings back the happiest childhood memories.

Granny's apple strudel

Serves 8
Preparation 40 minutes
Rest 1 hour
Cook 55 minutes

For the pastry
1 cup very fine or
    all-purpose flour
½ tsp salt
½ tbsp vinegar
1 tbsp oil
milk for brushing

For the filling
2¼lb (1kg) tart apples
    (e.g. Northern Spy)
1 tsp ground cinnamon
2 tbsp sugar
½ cup plus 3 tbsp raisins
    (adjust quantity to taste)
2 medium eggs
pinch of salt
7fl oz (200ml) sour cream
4 tbsp butter
¼ cup breadcrumbs

Special equipment
food processor
pastry cloth or large
    kitchen towel

Mix the flour and salt to make the pastry. Add the vinegar, oil, and 8 teaspoons of warm water, and slowly knead the ingredients using a food processor.

Gradually add another 6–8 teaspoons of water. After mixing, the pastry should be soft, elastic, and smooth so that you can stretch it out easily. Knead the pastry by hand on a floured work surface for another 10 minutes. Brush with oil, wrap in plastic wrap, and let it rest at room temperature for 1 hour.

Peel, core, and grate the apples for the filling. Mix in the cinnamon, sugar, and raisins, and set aside. Separate the eggs. Beat the egg whites with the salt until stiff. Stir the egg yolks into the sour cream. Fold in the beaten egg whites and set aside.

Preheat the oven to 400°F (200°C). Roll out the strudel pastry as thinly as possible on a lightly floured work surface. Every so often, turn the pastry over and dust with extra flour. Lightly dust a pastry cloth or kitchen towel with flour, and place the pastry on top. Slide your hands under the pastry with your palms down, and use the backs of your hands to pull and stretch the pastry very gradually from the center outward until you have created an extremely thin rectangle. Trim off any edges that are too thick.

Melt the butter, brush the pastry with it, and scatter over the breadcrumbs. Spread the apple filling in a line at one end of the pastry, leaving a gap of about 1¹/₂–2in (4–5cm) along both sides. Add dollops of the sour cream and egg mixture on top. Fold the sides of the pastry over the filling and roll up the strudel using the floured cloth or kitchen towel to help you.

Place the strudel seam-side down on a baking sheet lined with parchment paper. Brush with plenty of milk and bake in the oven on the middle shelf for 45–55 minutes. After about 30 minutes, brush it generously again with milk. Remove from the oven and serve lukewarm with custard or ice cream.

Cinnamon bun meets Bundt cake. This apple Bundt cake with a cinnamon and pecan swirl is irresistible. Apples are grated into the cake batter to keep it nice and moist.

Apple Bundt cake with a cinnamon and pecan swirl

Makes 1
Preparation 25 minutes
Cook 1 hour 10 minutes

For the cinnamon filling
¾ cup pecans
2 tbsp ground cinnamon
½ cup light brown sugar
breadcrumbs for the pan

For the cake mix
2 medium apples
    (e.g. Fuji, McIntosh)
16 tbsp soft butter, plus
    extra for greasing
⅔ cup granulated sugar
pinch of salt
zest of ½ organic lemon
1 tsp vanilla extract
4 medium eggs
2½ cups all-purpose flour
2 tsp baking powder
3½ tbsp milk
confectioner's sugar
    for dusting (optional)

Special equipment
food processor
9-cup swirl Bundt cake pan

Pulse the pecans in a food processor until finely ground. Add the cinnamon and sugar and combine. Preheat the oven to 350°F (180°C). Grease a Bundt pan and lightly sprinkle with breadcrumbs.

Peel, core, and grate the apples. Cream the butter with the sugar, salt, lemon zest, and vanilla extract until light and fluffy. Gradually add the eggs. Stir about a quarter of the flour, baking powder, and milk alternately into the butter and sugar mixture. Mix in the grated apples.

Put a quarter of the cake mix into the pan and smooth the surface. Sprinkle a third of the cinnamon filling on top, cover with a quarter of the cake mix, followed by another third of the cinnamon

filling. Repeat these layers, finishing with the last quarter of the cake mix. Bake in the oven on the bottom shelf for 1 hour to 1 hour 10 minutes. Insert a skewer into the center of the cake; if it comes out clean, the cake is done.

Remove the cake from the oven when ready and leave to cool slightly before turning it out of the pan. Allow it to cool completely on a wire rack. You can dust the cake with confectioner's sugar, if using, before serving.

Super chocolatey and super moist, this apple brownie cake is topped with sugared cinnamon almonds and offers everything you could want from a fine chocolate cake. The tart Northern Spy apples we use in our recipe complement the flavor of the dark chocolate beautifully.

Apple brownie cake

Makes 1 cake, 9½ or 10¼in (24 or 26cm) diameter
Preparation 25 minutes
Cook 50 minutes

For the cake mix
14 tbsp butter, plus extra for greasing
breadcrumbs for the pan
7oz (200g) dark chocolate
3–4 medium Northern Spy apples
3 large eggs
¾ cup granulated sugar
¾ cup plus 1 tbsp all-purpose flour
¼ cup cocoa powder
pinch of salt

For the almonds
¼ cup (20g) sliced almonds
½ tsp ground cinnamon
½ tbsp granulated sugar

Special equipment
9½ or 10¼in (24 or 26cm) springform pan
bain-marie (optional)

Preheat the oven to 350°F (180°C). Grease the bottom and sides of a cake pan and scatter with breadcrumbs.

Slice the butter into roughly ³/₄in (2cm) cubes. Cut the chocolate into pieces. Slowly melt both these ingredients over a bain-marie or in a bowl placed over a pan of simmering water. Remove from the stove and leave to cool to room temperature. Wash and core the apples and cut into wedges.

Whisk the eggs with the sugar in a mixing bowl until they are pale and creamy, and the whisk leaves a ribbon when lifted. Add the cooled chocolate and butter mixture and carefully fold it into the eggs using a spatula. Do not work the mixture any more than is necessary.

Sift the flour, cocoa, and salt into a bowl. Quickly fold these ingredients into the cake mix. Only stir as much as is needed to combine the ingredients. Transfer into the prepared pan and top with the slices of apple. Press the apples down slightly into the cake mix.

Bake in the oven on the middle shelf for 40–50 minutes. The brownie should still be slightly moist in the center.

Meanwhile, mix the almonds with the cinnamon and sugar, and toast them in a pan until golden brown and beginning to caramelize.

Remove the brownie from the oven, scatter with almonds, and serve.

Delicate apple roses make this a stunning dessert. Shaping the roses requires a little patience and skill, but it's worth the effort. The end result is both eye-catching and delicious.

Apple rose pie

Makes 1 pie, 8in (20cm)
  diameter
Preparation 45 minutes
Rest 1 hour
Cook 1 hour 5 minutes

For the pastry
9 tbsp cold butter, plus
  extra for greasing
1 cup plus 2 tbsp
  all-purpose flour
¼ tsp salt
1 heaped tbsp whole
  cane sugar
½ tsp apple vinegar
breadcrumbs for the pan
2¾ cups legumes or beans
  for blind baking, or
  ceramic or metal beans
  if preferred

For the filling
1 cup plus 2 tbsp
  apple butter (see p166)
  or sweet apple purée
2 large eggs
¾ cup heavy cream
1 tbsp cornstarch

For the apple roses
4 medium Gala apples
juice of ½ lemon
½ cup granulated sugar
confectioner's sugar
  for dusting

Special equipment
8in (20cm) diameter pie dish

To make the pastry, slice the butter into roughly ³/₄in (2cm) cubes and refrigerate. Combine the flour, salt, and sugar. Add the butter to the flour mixture and rub in swiftly. Add 2 tablespoons of ice-cold water and the vinegar to the pastry, and combine until the crumbs begin to stick together. If necessary, add another 1–2 tablespoons of ice-cold water.

Quickly shape the pastry into a ball on a floured work surface. You should still be able to see separate flecks of butter. Shape the pastry into a flat disk, wrap it in plastic wrap, and let it rest in the fridge for at least 1 hour. Stir together all the ingredients for the filling. Preheat the oven to 400°F (200°C).

Roll out the pastry on a floured work surface until it is about ¹/₈in (3–4mm) thick. Lightly grease a pie dish and scatter it with breadcrumbs. Transfer the pastry to the pie dish. Trim the edges of the pastry to create a uniform edge of about ³/₄in (2cm). Use your fingers to press the pastry into a fluted shape around the edges of the pan. Prick the base all over with a fork. Line with parchment paper and weigh this down with baking beans. Bake

blind for 10–15 minutes. Take the pastry out of the oven, leave to cool, and remove the baking beans and parchment paper. Set aside.

To make the apple roses, first wash, quarter, and core the apples. Slice them extremely thinly and drizzle with lemon juice. Heat the sugar in a pan with 1¹/₄ cups of water until the sugar has dissolved. Cook the apple slices in batches until they are soft enough to roll up but not falling apart. Scoop out the cooked apple slices and leave to cool. If necessary, add more water and sugar for the next batch.

Spread the filling over the pastry crust. Wrap the first slice of apple around your finger, and continue to wrap more apple slices until you have made a rose of the desired size. Put it into the filling. Repeat this process until you have filled the pie with apple roses.

Bake in the preheated oven on the middle shelf for 10 minutes, then lower the temperature to 350°F (180°C) and continue cooking for 35–40 minutes. Remove, leave to cool, and dust with confectioner's sugar.

Sunken apple cake with marzipan and a salted caramel sauce

Makes 1 cake, 9½in (24cm) diameter
Preparation 40 minutes
Cook 1 hour

For the cake mix
11 tbsp soft butter, plus extra for greasing
breadcrumbs for the pan
⅔ cup granulated sugar
1½ tsp vanilla extract
salt
2 medium eggs, beaten
3½oz (100g) marzipan
⅔ cup full-fat Greek yogurt
1½ cups plus 1 tbsp all-purpose flour
1 tsp baking powder
2–3 tbsp whole milk, if necessary
about 3 sweet and tangy apples (e.g. Northern Spy)
2–3 tbsp sliced almonds for sprinkling
confectioner's sugar for dusting

For the sauce
½ cup granulated sugar
¾ cup heavy cream
2 tbsp butter
1 tsp sea salt

Special equipment
9½in (24cm) springform pan

Preheat the oven to 350°F (180°C). Grease a springform pan and lightly scatter with breadcrumbs. Cream the butter, sugar, vanilla extract, and a pinch of salt for the cake mix. Stir in the eggs in two stages. Coarsely grate the marzipan. Add to the butter and sugar mixture, and beat until you have a creamy consistency. Add the yogurt and stir in briefly.

Combine the flour, baking powder, and a pinch of salt, sift these into the cake mix, and fold them in. The mixture should have a soft dropping consistency. If necessary, add some milk. Transfer into the prepared pan and smooth the surface.

Peel, quarter, and core the apples. Make multiple incisions on the curved side of each apple quarter, without slicing all the way through. Place the apple pieces in a spiral pattern, close together and with the curved sides facing up, pressing them gently into the cake mix. Bake in the preheated oven on the middle shelf for 1 hour until the apples are tender and the cake has cooked through. If the cake starts browning too quickly, cover it with foil.

Meanwhile, make the salted caramel sauce. Slowly caramelize the sugar in a pan over a moderate heat. Add the heavy cream, butter, and sea salt. Stir over a low heat until you have a thick sauce. The sauce will continue to thicken as it cools, so don't let it thicken too much before turning off the heat.

Remove the apple cake from the oven and leave to cool. Release the cake from the pan, scatter with sliced almonds, and dust with confectioner's sugar. Serve with the sauce. Any leftover sauce will keep well for several days if stored in the fridge in a sealed container.

Gâteau with a caramelized apple filling

Makes 1 cake, 6¼in (16cm)
   diameter
Preparation 1½ hours
Cook 40 minutes

For the cake
4 medium eggs
pinch of salt
⅓ cup granulated sugar
1 tsp organic lemon zest
½ cup all-purpose flour
3 tbsp plus 1 tsp cornstarch
½ tsp baking powder

For the icing
10 tbsp soft butter
½ cup plus 3 tbsp
   confectioner's sugar
10oz (300g) full-fat
   cream cheese
1lb 2oz (500g) quark
2 tbsp maple syrup
½ tsp ground cinnamon
pinch of ground ginger
zest of ½ organic lemon

For the filling
½ cup sliced almonds
2 Jonagold apples
¼ cup granulated sugar
¼ vanilla bean
½ tsp ground cinnamon

For decoration
1 Jonagold apple
lemon juice
2 tbsp almonds
4 cinnamon sticks
4 star anise
maple syrup for drizzling

Special equipment
6¼in (16cm) springform pan
piping bag and nozzle

Preheat the oven to 350°F
180°C). Line a pan with
parchment paper. Separate
the eggs. Whisk the egg whites
with the salt until stiff, sprinkling
in half the sugar as you go. In
a separate bowl, whisk the egg
yolks with the remaining sugar
and lemon zest for about
4 minutes until the mixture
is pale and creamy.

Sift together the flour, cornstarch,
and baking powder in a separate
bowl. Fold the whisked egg
whites into the egg yolk mixture
in two batches. Carefully and
quickly fold in the flour in two
batches. Transfer the mixture into
the pan and bake in the oven on
the middle shelf for 30–40
minutes. Remove, leave to cool
briefly, and carefully loosen the
edges with a knife. Leave to cool
completely on a wire rack and
then slice horizontally into three
equal layers.

To make the icing, cream the
butter and icing sugar until light
and fluffy. Gradually stir in the
cream cheese. Add the quark,
maple syrup, cinnamon, ginger,
and lemon zest, and mix
everything briefly. Refrigerate.

Toast the sliced almonds for the
filling. Set aside. Peel and core
the apples and chop into small
cubes. Caramelize the sugar with
3 tablespoons of water in a pan.
Slice the vanilla bean in half
lengthways and scrape out the
seeds. Add these to the pan
along with the apples and
cinnamon, and simmer over a
moderate heat until the apples
are soft. Finally, fold in the sliced
almonds and set aside.

Set aside 3–4 tablespoons of the
icing and put the rest into a
piping bag. Pipe a ring of icing
around the edge of two of the
three cake layers. Spread the
apple filling in the center, pipe
some icing on top of the filling,
and smooth it over. Stack the
cake layers on a large plate.
Spread some of the reserved
icing over the top and sides of
the gâteau smoothly, and then
chill it for 30 minutes. Spread
the rest of the icing on smoothly.

Wash, quarter, and core the
apple for decoration. Cut eight
thin slices, drizzle with lemon
juice, and arrange these in a
semicircle on top of the gâteau.
Roughly chop the almonds.
Decorate with cinnamon sticks,
star anise, and almonds. Drizzle
with maple syrup before serving.

This Florentine apple cake owes its name to the layer of caramelized almonds, inspired by the Florentine biscuit. The almonds add a really special touch, harmonizing beautifully with apples that have a balance of both sweet and acidic flavours, such as Cortland, Honeycrisp, or Northern Spy.

Florentine apple cake

Makes 1 cake, 9½ or 10¼in (24 or 26cm) diameter
Preparation 25 minutes
Rest 1 hour
Cook 55 minutes

For the pastry
11 tbsp soft butter
½ cup confectioner's sugar
1½ tsp vanilla extract
pinch of salt
1 medium egg
1¾ cups plus 2 tbsp
   all-purpose flour

For the filling
2¼lb (1kg) sweet and tangy
   apples (see above)
juice of ½ lemon
1 tsp ground cinnamon
½ tsp ground cardamom
1–2 tbsp granulated sugar

For the glaze
7 tbsp butter
½ cup granulated sugar
1½ tbsp all-purpose flour
⅓ cup heavy cream
1¾ cup (190g) sliced almonds

Special equipment
food processor
9½ or 10¼in (24 or 26cm
   springform pan)

For the pastry, briefly mix the butter, confectioner's sugar, vanilla extract, and salt in a food processor using the dough hook. Add the egg and flour and process the mixture as briefly as possible until it begins to combine. The pastry should be coming away from the sides of the bowl and not be too sticky. Use your hands to bring the pastry smoothly together on a lightly floured work surface and shape it into a flat disk. Wrap in plastic wrap and let it rest in the fridge for at least 1 hour.

Peel, core, and cut the apples into eight segments each. Slice these thinly, transfer to a bowl, and mix well with the lemon juice, cinnamon, cardamom, and 1–2 tablespoons of sugar (depending on the tartness of the apples). Preheat the oven to 350°F (180°C).

Remove the pastry from the fridge and leave it for a few minutes until you can roll it out easily. Roll the pastry on a floured work surface to a thickness of roughly $1/16$–$1/8$in (2–3mm). Line a pan with the pastry, pressing it in place with your fingers. Prick the base all over with a fork and transfer the pan to the fridge.

Heat the butter and sugar for the glaze in a pan. Stir in the flour and remove from the stove. Stir in the heavy cream and sliced almonds.

Spread the apple filling over the pastry base and cover with the almond glaze. Bake in the preheated oven for 50–55 minutes until the almonds are golden and slightly caramelized. Remove from the oven and let cool completely.

Light, fluffy quark with a rich cream topping: this easy apple torte is unbeatable.
You don't even have to bake a separate base for this cake—the quark mixture contains
semolina and cornstarch, creating a stable structure for a deliciously light base.

Apple and quark torte

**Makes 1 torte, 11in (28cm)
    diameter**
Preparation 20 minutes
Cook 1½ hours

For the base
1lb 2oz (500g apples)
    Cortland, Northern Spy)
zest and juice of 1 organic
    lemon
9 tbsp soft butter
1 cup plus 2 tbsp
    granulated sugar
2 tsp vanilla extract
5 medium eggs
⅔ cup full-fat Greek yogurt
2¼lb (1kg) quark (can sub
    cream cheese or ricotta
2 tbsp semolina
⅓ cup (40g) cornstarch

For the topping
1¾ cups heavy cream
1½ tsp vanilla extract
2 medium apples (e.g.
    Cortland, Northern Spy)
juice of ½ lemon
¼ cup hazelnuts

Special equipment
11in (28cm) springform pan
electric hand mixer
piping bag and star-shaped
    nozzle

Peel, core, and grate the apples.
Mix the lemon zest and juice with
the apples.

Preheat the oven to 325°F
(170°C). Line the base of a pan
with parchment paper.

Cream the butter, sugar, and
vanilla extract with a hand mixer.
Gradually add the eggs. Stir in
the yogurt and quark until you
have a creamy consistency.
Combine the semolina and
cornstarch, and fold into the
quark mixture. Add the grated
apples and fold into the mix.

Transfer the mixture to the
prepared pan, spread it
smoothly, and bake in the oven
on the middle shelf for 1½ hours.
Turn off the oven and let
it stand with the door slightly
open for 10 minutes. Remove
from the oven and leave to
cool completely on a wire
rack. Release from the pan.

To make the topping, whisk the
heavy cream with the vanilla
extract until stiff. Set aside a
small amount, spreading the rest
over the cooled torte. Put the
rest of the heavy cream into
a piping bag with a large star-
shaped nozzle and pipe 12
small swirls on the top.

Shortly before serving, wash the
apples, slice 12 thin slices from
the whole fruit, and drizzle with
lemon juice to stop them going
brown. Put one slice into each
of the piped swirls of cream.
Roughly chop the hazelnuts and
sprinkle over. Ideally, serve the
torte well chilled.

Doughnuts with an apple and custard filling

Makes about 12
Preparation 50 minutes
Rest 1 hour 45 minutes

For the mix
¾ cup milk
2¾ cups plus 1 tbsp
   all-purpose flour
1 ¼oz (7g) packet active dry
   yeast
¼ cup granulated sugar,
   divided
5 tbsp butter
pinch of salt
1 medium egg
1 tsp organic orange zest
4¼ cups vegetable oil
sugar for coating

For the filling
1 medium apple
1 tbsp lemon juice
2 tsp granulated sugar
½ tsp ground cinnamon
pinch of ground cardamom
2 tsp cornstarch

For the custard
⅓ vanilla bean
¾ cup milk
2 tbsp plus 1 tsp sugar
2 tbsp cornstarch
1 medium egg yolk

Special equipment
handheld blender
cooking thermometer
piping bag and long, narrow
   nozzle

Warm the milk in a small pan. Put the flour in a bowl and make a well in the center. Sprinkle the yeast into the well, add 1 teaspoon of sugar, then pour in the milk. Whisk in a little flour from the sides until the yeast has dissolved. Cover and let it stand for about 15 minutes.

Melt the butter and leave to cool. Add this to the yeast and milk mixture with 3 tablespoons plus 2 teaspoons of sugar, salt, egg, and orange zest. Knead everything together until the dough is smooth. Cover and leave to proof for at least 1 hour.

Roll the dough out on a floured work surface to a thickness of $^3/_4$–$1^1/_4$in (2–3cm) and cut out circles measuring $2^3/_4$–3in (7–8cm) in diameter. Space these slightly apart on a baking sheet lined with parchment paper, cover, and let it proof for another 30 minutes.

To make the filling, wash, core, and finely chop the apple. Add to a pan with the lemon juice, sugar, cinnamon, cardamom, and 1 cup plus 2 tablespoons of water, and simmer for about 10 minutes over a moderate heat.

Mix 2 tablespoons of water with the cornstarch until smooth. Add this to the pan, bring to a boil, stirring constantly, and then let it cool. If desired, reserve 2–3 tablespoons as decoration. Use a handheld blender to purée the rest until smooth.

To make the custard, scrape the seeds out of the vanilla bean. Add the seeds, bean, and milk to a pan. Take 2 tablespoons of milk from the pan and stir this into the sugar and cornstarch. Bring the milk to a boil, add the cornstarch mixture, and stir constantly to return briefly to a boil. Remove from the stove, stir in the egg yolk, and let it cool.

Heat the oil in a pan until it reaches a temperature of 338°F (170°C). Add the doughnuts to the hot oil. Cover and cook for about 2–3 minutes. Remove the lid, turn the doughnuts, and continue cooking for another 2–3 minutes, or until a skewer inserted comes out clean. Lift the doughnuts out of the oil, drain on paper towel, then toss in sugar to coat. Use a piping bag with a long, narrow nozzle to fill the doughnuts, first with the puréed apple and then with the custard.

This is an essential recipe in any apple cookbook. Apple fritters with cinnamon and sugar bring back all sorts of childhood memories for us. Our tip: use an older, fairly tart variety of apple. This will make your fritters taste just like granny used to make them.

Apple fritters with cinnamon and sugar

Serves 4
Preparation 30 minutes

1¼ cups plus 2 tbsp 00 flour
   or white spelt flour
2 medium eggs
2 pinches of salt
½ cup plus 3 tbsp granulated
   sugar
¾ cup milk
2¼ tsp ground cinnamon
4 apples (e.g. Honeycrisp,
   Northern Spy)
about ¾ cup vegetable oil for
   frying (depending on the
   size of the pan)

Stir the flour, eggs, salt, 3 tablespoons plus 2 teaspoons of sugar, milk, and ¼ teaspoon of cinnamon together until you have a smooth batter. Wash the apples, remove the core, and slice them into ¼–½in- (0.5–1cm-) thick rings.

Pour oil into a pan to a depth of ½–⅝in (1–1.5cm) and heat. To test whether the oil is hot enough, put the handle of a wooden spoon into it. The oil has reached the right temperature if small bubbles form around the handle and rise to the surface. Combine the remaining 2 teaspoons of cinnamon and

¼ cup plus 3 tablespoons of sugar on a plate.

Toss the apple rings in the batter, let the batter drip off briefly, then fry the rings in the oil on both sides until golden. Finally, toss them in the cinnamon and sugar mixture. Enjoy them warm, perhaps with a serving of heavy cream, compote, or ice cream.

Making doughnuts from the first cider of the year is something of a tradition in the United States. The sparkling apple cider is brought to a boil and reduced, removing the alcohol from the liquid and imparting a lightness and delicious moistness to the doughnuts.

Apple cider doughnuts

Makes about 12
Preparation 40 minutes
Cook 10 minutes

For the doughnuts
1½ cups hard cider
1½ cups plus 1 tbsp
    all-purpose flour
1 tsp baking soda
¾ tsp baking powder
1 tsp ground cinnamon
pinch of ground cloves
½ tsp ground cardamom
pinch of ground ginger
¼ tsp salt
1 large egg
¼ cup plus 1 tbsp dark brown
    sugar
¼ cup granulated sugar
2 tbsp soft butter,
    plus extra for greasing
½ tsp vanilla extract
⅓–½ cup buttermilk

For the coating
6 tbsp butter
about ¾ cup plus 3 tbsp
    granulated sugar
1½–2 tsp ground cinnamon

Special equipment
doughnut pan
disposable piping bag

Bring the cider to a boil in a small pan. Simmer over a moderate heat for 20–25 minutes and reduce to about ¼ cup plus 3 tablespoons. Remove from the stove and let it cool.

Preheat the oven to 350°F (180°C). Grease the mold in a doughnut tray. Set aside.

Combine the flour, baking soda, baking powder, cinnamon, cloves, cardamom, ginger, and salt in a bowl.

Beat the egg with the brown and granulated sugar, butter, and vanilla extract until pale and creamy. Quickly stir in the cooled cider. Alternately add some of the flour mixture and buttermilk, stirring everything swiftly to a smooth consistency. Do not overwork the mixture.

Transfer the mixture into a disposable piping bag and snip off the end. Fill the doughnut molds about two-thirds full. Bake in a preheated oven on the middle shelf for about 10 minutes. Test to see if the doughnuts are done—an inserted skewer should come out clean. Remove from the oven, leave to cool for 5 minutes, and turn them out onto a wire rack. Leave to cool completely.

Melt the butter for coating the doughnuts in a small pan. Combine the sugar and cinnamon in a bowl. First dunk each doughnut into the butter, let the butter drip off slightly, and then toss it in the sugar and cinnamon mixture. They are best enjoyed freshly cooked.

Crisp on the outside, light and delicate on the inside—that's how we think the perfect waffle should be. Adding apple purée to the batter makes this delicious treat even moister. A single bite, and we are in food heaven.

Apple purée waffles with caramelized apples

Serves 4
Preparation 30 minutes

For the waffles
7 tbsp soft butter
3 tbsp plus 2 tsp granulated
  sugar
2 medium eggs
1¼ cups 00 flour or white
  spelt flour
pinch of salt
1 tsp baking powder
½ cup plus 1 tbsp milk
¼ cup plus 3 tbsp apple
  purée (see p174)
½ tsp ground cinnamon
oil for brushing

For the apples
1 apple (e.g. Honeycrisp)
1 tbsp butter
2 tbsp granulated sugar
¼ cup maple syrup

Special equipment
waffle iron

Use a balloon whisk to combine the butter, sugar, eggs, flour, salt, baking powder, milk, apple purée, and cinnamon until you have a smooth batter. Let it stand briefly. Meanwhile, heat up a waffle iron.

Wash the apple and slice into thin rings. Melt the butter in a pan. Fry the apple rings on both sides, sprinkle with sugar, and allow to caramelize.

Brush the waffle iron with a little oil and cook the waffles until golden. Top with slices of apple and drizzle with maple syrup. These waffles are delicious served with vanilla ice cream or heavy cream.

Apple and cinnamon swirls with caramelized sunflower seeds

Makes 12–15
Preparation 40 minutes
Rest 1 hour 45 minutes
Cook 20 minutes

For the dough
¾ cup plus 1 tbsp milk
2¾ cup plus 1 tbsp white
    spelt flour
1 ¼oz (7g) packet active
    dried yeast
¼ cup plus 2 tbsp sugar
6 tbsp butter
pinch of salt
1 large egg (room temp.)

For the seeds
½ cup plus 3 tbsp sunflower
    seeds
1 medium egg white
¼ cup granulated sugar
1 tsp ground cinnamon

For the filling
3 large apples
juice of ½ lemon
6 tbsp butter
¼ cup plus 2 tbsp whole cane
    sugar
1 tsp ground cinnamon
½ tsp ground cardamom

For the icing
3½oz (100g) full-fat cream
    cheese
4 tbsp soft butter
¾ cup plus 2 tbsp
    confectioner's sugar
1 tbsp milk

Heat the milk until lukewarm, put the flour in a bowl, and make a well in the center. Sprinkle the yeast into the well, add the sugar, and pour in the milk. Whisk in a little flour from the sides until the yeast has dissolved. Cover and let it stand for 15 minutes.

Meanwhile, melt the butter and let it cool until lukewarm. Add this to the yeast mixture along with the salt and egg, then knead everything to an elastic dough. Cover and leave to proof for 1 hour until doubled in volume.

To toast the seeds, preheat the oven to 400°F (200°C). Combine all the ingredients with 1 teaspoon of water and spread out over a baking sheet lined with parchment paper. Bake for 10–15 minutes until golden. Toss the seeds occasionally during cooking. Remove from the oven and leave to cool.

To make the filling, wash and core the apples, chop into roughly $^1/_4$in (5mm) cubes, and drizzle with lemon juice. Heat 1 tablespoon of butter in a pan, and fry the apples until soft but not mushy. Pour off any liquid that is released. Add the rest of the butter, allow it to melt, and remove from the stove. In a bowl, combine the cane sugar, cinnamon, and cardamom, and set aside.

Roll out the dough on a floured work surface to make a 32 x 24in (80 x 60cm) rectangle. Spread with the apple mixture, leaving about a 4in- (10cm-) wide gap along the long edge at the top. Sprinkle the apples with the cinnamon and sugar mixture. Brush the top edge of the dough with water and roll it up from the bottom long edge. Place the roll seam-side down and slice into $^3/_4$–1$^1/_2$in- (2–4cm-) wide pieces. Lay these out flat on a baking sheet lined with parchment paper. Cover and leave to proof for a further 30 minutes.

Preheat the oven to 350°F (180°C) and bake the spirals for about 20 minutes until golden.

Stir together all the ingredients for the icing and spread it over the apple spirals. Sprinkle with sunflower seeds.

With a crunchy crust and fluffy white crumb, these potato rolls with apples and walnuts taste as if they were made by your local bakery, but even inexperienced bakers can easily rustle them up. We recommend making a large batch and freezing some.

Potato rolls with apples and walnuts

Makes 16 rolls
Preparation 30 minutes
Rest 12½ hours
Cook 25 minutes

8½oz (240g) russet potatoes
4 cups plus 2 tbsp
    all-purpose flour, plus
    extra for working
1 cup plus 3 tbsp dark rye
    flour
2 packets (½oz/14g) instant
    dried yeast
2½oz (75g) sourdough
    starter (available online
    or make your own)
2 tsp salt
1 tsp granulated sugar
2 tbsp vegetable oil
1⅓ cups walnuts
1 large apple, about
    7oz (200g) e.g. Idared,
    McIntosh)

Special equipment
baking stone (optional)

Peel the potatoes and cook until soft. Leave to cool slightly and mash well with a ricer or potato masher. Combine both kinds of flour, yeast, sourdough starter, salt, sugar, oil, and 1^1/$_4$ cups of water, and knead for 10 minutes until you have a smooth dough. Cover and leave the dough to proof in a bowl at room temperature for 8–12 hours (ideally overnight).

Chop the walnuts. Wash, core, and cube the apple. Knead the dough on a well-floured work surface, working in the chopped apple and walnuts. Shape the dough into a long log and cut into 16 equal-sized portions. Shape the pieces of dough into balls and make an incision in each with a sharp knife. Cover and leave to proof at room temperature for 30 minutes. Dust with flour.

Meanwhile, preheat the oven to 450°F (230°C). The rolls are best cooked on a baking stone or you can use a baking sheet. Slide a dripping pan or deep baking sheet into the oven to heat up. Just before you put the rolls in to cook, carefully pour about 3^1/$_2$ tablespoons of hot water into the pan or deep baking sheet. Slide the rolls into the oven on the middle shelf above the pan or deep baking sheet, and shut the door immediately to prevent steam from escaping. Bake the rolls in the oven for 20 minutes.

Remove the deep baking sheet or dripping pan, let the steam escape, and cook the rolls for a further 5 minutes until crisp.

For a delicious breakfast, we recommend you serve these rolls with our apple and ginger jelly (see p177).

This is a very special rye and wheat loaf with a particularly fine crumb and a wonderful sharp tang. It's packed with flavor and stays fresh for a long time. The cider vinegar in the dough helps intensify the distinctive sourdough taste, but don't worry, you won't be able to detect the vinegar once the bread is cooked.

Rye and wheat bread with cider vinegar

Makes 1 loaf
Preparation 30 minutes
Rest 15 hours
Cook 55 minutes

For the sourdough
1½ cups plus 2 tbsp medium
  to dark rye flour
1oz (30g) sourdough starter
  (available online or make
  your own)

For the yeast starter
¾ cup bread flour with a
  high gluten content
¼ tsp active dry yeast

For the main dough
1¾ cups plus 3 tbsp medium
  to dark rye flour, plus
  extra for kneading
1 tbsp salt
1¾ tsp active dry yeast
1 tsp bread spice (see
  Tip, right)
1 tbsp cider vinegar
  (see p164)

Special equipment
proofing basket (optional)
baking stone (optional)

To make the sourdough, combine the flour with 1 cup plus 2 tablespoons of lukewarm water and the sourdough starter in a bowl. For the yeast starter, combine the flour, $^1/_2$ cup of water, and yeast in another bowl. Cover both bowls and leave to proof overnight at room temperature.

The next day, combine all the ingredients for the main dough with $^1/_4$ cup of water, the sourdough, and yeast starter in a large mixing bowl. Knead together for 10 minutes. Shape the dough into a round on a well-floured work surface. Put the dough seam-side down in a proofing basket or a bowl lined with a floured cotton cloth, and leave to proof at room temperature for 1 hour. Preheat the oven to 500°F (250°C).

The bread is best cooked on a baking stone or you can use a baking sheet. Slide a dripping pan or deep baking sheet into the oven to heat up. Just before you put the bread in to bake, carefully pour about $3^1/_2$ tablespoons of hot water into the pan or deep baking sheet. Put the loaf into the oven on the middle shelf above the pan or deep baking sheet, and shut the door immediately to prevent steam from escaping. Bake the bread for 15 minutes.

Remove the deep baking sheet or pan if it still contains water, let the steam escape, and continue baking for a further 40 minutes at 350°F (160°C). Leave it to rest for 1–2 hours after baking.

Tip: Make your own bread spice by finely grinding fennel, coriander, caraway, cardamom, anise, and blue fenugreek.

DESSERTS, SMALL BITES, AND DRINKS

Apple ice cream with thyme and an amaretti crumble

DESSERTS, SMALL BITES, AND DRINKS

Serves 4
Preparation 30 minutes

1¾oz (50g) tart apple (e.g.
  Granny Smith), plus
  ½ apple for garnish
1¼ cups sour cream
¾ cup heavy cream
¼ cup plus 2 tbsp granulated
  sugar
juice of 1 lime
2 sprigs of thyme
1 tbsp Calvados (apple
  brandy)
5–6 amaretti biscuits,
  crushed

Special equipment
ice-cream maker (optional)

Wash and core the apple, and grate about 1³/₄oz (50g). Combine the sour cream and heavy cream in a bowl with the grated apple and sugar. Add the lime juice to the cream mixture. Wash and shake dry the thyme and strip off the leaves, setting a couple aside for garnish. Fold the thyme and Calvados into the mixture. Transfer to an ice-cream maker and freeze until it reaches the desired consistency. Finely chop ¹/₂ apple. Sprinkle the ice cream with amaretti crumbs, thyme leaves, and diced apple to serve.

If you do not have an ice-cream maker, put the mixture into a shallow container, cover, and put in the freezer until an inch or two (a few centimeters) of the mixture has frozen around the edge. Depending on the size of the container and the temperature of your freezer, this may take 60–90 minutes.

Remove the ice cream from the freezer and beat it vigorously with a balloon whisk to break up the frozen section around the edge. Beat plenty of air in to get a smooth consistency. Return the container to the freezer and repeat this process two or three times at shorter intervals until the ice cream has reached the desired consistency.

Apple mousse with chocolate crumble

Makes 6 x 7fl oz (200ml) ramekins
Preparation 25 minutes
Chill 2–3 hours
Cook 10 minutes

For the mousse
¾ cup apple juice, divided
5 tsp powdered gelatin
3 sweet apples (e.g. Gala, Golden Delicious)
2 sage leaves
1 tbsp honey
1¼ cups heavy cream

For the crumble
3 tbsp cocoa powder
¼ cup plus 3 tbsp ground almonds
½ cup plus 1 tbsp all-purpose flour
¼ cup plus 1 tbsp granulated sugar
pinch of salt
4 tbsp cold butter, diced

Special equipment
handheld blender

Pour $^1/_2$ cup of apple juice into a medium bowl, sprinkle gelatin on top, and let it stand for 5–10 minutes. Wash, core, and roughly chop the apples. Wash, shake dry, and chop the sage. Put this in a pan with the apples, $^1/_4$ cup of apple juice, and honey. Bring to a boil, stirring constantly. Simmer for 10–15 minutes until the apples are soft and some of the liquid has been reduced. Remove from the stove and use a handheld blender to purée.

Add the softened gelatin mixture to the still-warm apple purée and blend until smooth. Let cool,

stirring occasionally. Whip the cream until stiff and fold it into the cooled purée. Decant the mousse into glasses and chill for 2–3 hours in the fridge until set.

Preheat the oven to 400°F (200°C). To make the crumble, combine the cocoa powder, almonds, flour, sugar, salt, and butter in a bowl, and rub it together with your fingers to create a crumble. Spread this out on a baking sheet lined with parchment paper and bake for 8–10 minutes. Leave to cool and sprinkle over the mousse.

Sorbet is how ice cream originated, and recipes for this dessert date back to ancient times. A classic sorbet uses only water and sugar in addition to the fruit juice. We have used the Granny Smith apple here as it has such an intensely tangy and fresh flavor.

Apple sorbet

Serves 4
Preparation 1 hour

2 Granny Smith apples,
    about 9oz (250g)
juice of 1 lemon
¼ cup plus 3 tbsp granulated
    sugar

Special equipment
food processor or blender
ice-cream maker (optional)

Wash, quarter, and core the apples. Chop into large chunks and put these in a food processor or blender. Add the lemon juice to the apples with the sugar and ³/₄ cup plus 1 tablespoon of water. Purée until you have a smooth mixture. Transfer into an ice-cream maker and freeze until it reaches the desired consistency.

If you do not have an ice-cream maker, put the mixture into a shallow container, cover, and put in the freezer until an inch or two (a few centimeters) of the mixture has frozen around the edge. Depending on the size of the container and the temperature of your freezer, this may take 60–90 minutes.

Remove the sorbet from the freezer and beat it vigorously with a balloon whisk to break up the frozen section around the edge. Beat plenty of air in to get a smooth consistency. Return the container to the freezer and repeat this process two or three times at shorter intervals until the sorbet has reached the desired consistency.

Fruity, sweet, and creamy—that's how we like our trifle. This layered dessert consists of three components: traditionally, these are cream, cake, and fruit. In our recipe, we use layers of apple compote, ladyfingers soaked in hard cider, and a combination of quark and cream.

Apple trifle

Serves 4
Preparation 40 minutes

For the compote
1lb 9oz (700g) apples (e.g. Northern Spy, Fuji)
1 vanilla bean
½ cup plus 2 tbsp hard cider
1 cinnamon stick
1–2 tbsp honey
1 tsp ground cinnamon
½ tsp ground cardamom

For the filling
8 ladyfingers
¼ cup plus 2–3 tbsp hard cider
1 cup plus 1 tbsp heavy cream
13oz (375g) quark (can substitute cream cheese)
3 tbsp granulated sugar
apple chips (see p170) to serve
apple and cinnamon granola (see p169) to serve

Peel, quarter, core, and cube the apples for the compote. Slice the vanilla bean in half lengthways and scrape out the seeds. Add the seeds and pod to a pan with the apples, cider, cinnamon stick, honey, ground cinnamon, and cardamom. Bring briefly to a boil and simmer over a moderate heat until the apples are soft but not overcooked. Remove from the stove, discard the vanilla bean and cinnamon stick, and leave to cool.

Slice the ladyfingers in half and drizzle with the cider. Beat the heavy cream until semi-stiff. Combine the quark and sugar and stir well. Fold in the heavy cream.

Arrange alternating layers of cream, ladyfingers, and compote in the serving glasses. Refrigerate for at least 2 hours. Decorate with apple chips and granola to serve.

*These sweet and fruity fair favorites are easy to make at home,
and you can use a variety of different toppings, depending on your
taste. Use twigs as skewers to give this delicious treat a unique look.*

Toffee apples

DESSERTS, SMALL BITES, AND DRINKS

Serves 4
Preparation 30 minutes

2 tbsp chopped nuts,
    coconut flakes, hazelnut
    brittle, or chocolate
    sprinkles for each apple
4 tart apples (e.g. Fuji,
    Northern Spy)
4 wooden skewers or
    short, clean twigs
1 cup brown sugar (light or
    dark)
2 tbsp butter

Put your chosen toppings into
small bowls and set aside. Wash
the apples in hot water and dry
them carefully. Remove the stalks
and insert four skewers or twigs
halfway inside the apples.

Put the sugar and $^3/_4$ cup plus
1 tablespoon of water in a pan
and set over a moderate heat
until the sugar has dissolved. Add
the butter and continue cooking
until the mixture has caramelized.
To test if the toffee has reached
the right consistency, take a
small amount and drop it into a
glass of water. It should harden
immediately. Remove the pan
from the stove and transfer
the toffee mixture into a bowl.

Carefully dip the apples one
at a time in the hot toffee
mixture, turning them so they
are coated all over. Allow any
excess toffee to drip off by
turning the apples. Place the
apples on parchment paper
and let them cool slightly. While
the toffee is still soft, dip the
apples in the toppings. Return
them to the parchment paper
until completely set.

The smell of freshly baked apples is mouthwatering. The fruit goes wonderfully well with a filling of marzipan and raisins, and an oat-crumble topping adds a delicious crunch. You might like to serve this with custard or ice cream.

Baked apples with a marzipan filling and oat crumble

Serves 4
Preparation 15 minutes
Cook 30 minutes

For the crumble
1 tbsp plus 2 tsp hazelnuts
¼ cup (40g) oat flour
2 tbsp plus 2 tsp whole cane
    sugar
½ tsp ground cinnamon
3 tbsp white spelt flour
2 tbsp soft butter

For the apples
4 large, firm apples
    (e.g. Fuji, Northern
    Spy, Jonagold, Idared,
    Pink Lady)
1¾oz (50g) marzipan
3 tbsp plus 1 tsp raisins

Add all the ingredients for the crumble to a bowl and rub them together with your fingers until you have a crumbly consistency. Transfer to the fridge. Preheat the oven to 375°F (190°C).

Wash the apples and slice off the tops as lids. Cut out the core and some of the surrounding fruit to make a generous cavity. Put the apples in a baking dish.

Chop the marzipan into 12 equal-sized pieces. Put three pieces of marzipan and about 1 teaspoon of raisins into each apple cavity. Sprinkle a generous quantity of crumble over the apples. Bake in the oven on the middle shelf for 25–30 minutes, depending on the variety of apple, until the apples are soft but not overcooked.

Guilt-free snacks, these delicious apple balls are a healthy and delicious treat. Cinnamon and a dash of nutmeg give them a flavor reminiscent of apple pie. They are best eaten well chilled.

Apple pie energy balls

Makes 15
Preparation 15 minutes

1 medium sweet apple
   (e.g. Jonagold, Gala,
   Golden Delicious)
10 dried dates, about
   2¼oz (65g)
1¾oz (50g) dried apple rings
⅓ cup almonds
1 tsp ground cinnamon
pinch of freshly grated
   nutmeg
2 tbsp almond nut butter
1 tbsp coconut oil
¼ cup plus 1 tbsp oat flour
1–2 tbsp ground almonds
   (almond meal) for coating

Special equipment
food processor

Wash, core, and chop the apple. Put all the ingredients except the ground almonds in a food processor. Process until you have a sticky mixture. Take 1 tablespoon of the mixture and roll it into a ball with damp hands. Repeat for the rest of the mixture.

Put the ground almonds in a bowl and toss the balls in them. Keep the energy balls in the fridge.

If you crave snacks between meals but don't want to resort to chocolate or sweets, our muesli bars with apple purée and honey offer a healthy alternative. They are quick to make and can be stored for several days in an airtight container.

Apple muesli bars

**Makes 1 8 x 12in
(20 x 30cm) pan
Preparation 15 minutes
Cook 35 minutes**

1½–2 sweet apples
(e.g. Jonagold, McIntosh)
4 tbsp butter
3 tbsp honey
¼ cup apple sauce or
unsweetened apple purée
(see p174)
1 cup plus 2 tbsp oat flour
2 tbsp pumpkin seeds
1 tsp ground cinnamon
¼ tsp ground cardamom
pinch of salt

Special equipment
8 x 12in (20 x 30cm)
baking pan

Preheat the oven to 400°F (200°C). Line a pan with parchment paper.

Wash and core the apples. Grate one and cut the rest into thin slices.

Melt the butter in a small pan over a moderate heat. Stir in the honey and remove from the stove. Add the grated apple, apple sauce or purée, oats, pumpkin seeds, cinnamon, cardamom, and salt, and stir to combine. Transfer the mixture into the pan and press down firmly with the back of a spoon. Top with slices of apple, pressing them down into the mixture slightly with your fingers.

Bake in the oven on the middle shelf for 30–35 minutes until golden. Remove from the oven, allow to cool for 15 minutes, and remove from the pan. Use a sharp knife to cut into equal-sized bars. These bars can be kept for up to 4 days in an airtight container.

The Moscow mule is one of our favorite cocktails. The original is made using vodka, ginger beer, and lime juice. Our version uses hard cider, sliced apple, and a touch of cinnamon for a fabulously fruity flavor.

Apple cider Moscow mule

Serves 4
Preparation 10 minutes

4 sprigs of rosemary
2 limes
ice cubes
1¼ cups hard cider
2 cups ginger beer
1 cup vodka
pinch of ground cinnamon
apple slices for garnish
4 cinnamon sticks
    for garnish

Wash and shake dry the rosemary. Halve the limes. Divide the ice cubes between the tumblers and squeeze the juice of ½ lime into each.

Mix the cider, ginger beer, vodka, and cinnamon. Pour the mixture into the tumblers and stir well. Garnish each drink with a sprig of rosemary, some apple slices, and a cinnamon stick.

This apple and ginger spritzer is the perfect refreshing beverage for your next party. The ginger syrup can be prepared in advance, then mixed with prosecco, apple juice, and mineral water just before festivities start.

Apple and ginger spritzer

Serves 4
Preparation 15 minutes

For the ginger syrup
Scant 1oz (25g) ginger
1 sprig of rosemary
¼ cup plus 3 tbsp granulated
   sugar

For the spritzer
1 organic lemon
½ apple (e.g. Northern Spy)
ice cubes
3 cups prosecco
¾ cup plus 1 tbsp apple
   juice
mineral water for
   topping off
rosemary to serve (optional)

Peel and finely grate the ginger for the syrup. Wash and shake dry the rosemary. Add the ginger, rosemary, sugar, and ¼ cup plus 3 tablespoons of water to a pan, and simmer for 5–10 minutes until you have a thick syrup. Remove from the stove and leave to cool.

Wash and dry the lemon and apple and cut 4 thin slices from each. Remove the seeds from the apple slices and drizzle with lemon juice. Divide the ice cubes between four wine glasses or cocktail glasses and pour over the syrup. Divide the prosecco and apple juice between the glasses and top up with mineral water as desired. Add the sliced apple and lemon. Serve garnished with rosemary, if using.

For a real boost at the start of your day, we recommend our apple and spinach smoothie. This healthy shake contains a large dose of vitamin C as well as betacarotene, which the body converts into vitamin A. Among other things, vitamin A is vital for healthy eyes, skin, bones, and teeth.

Apple and spinach smoothie

Serves about 4
Preparation 10 minutes

3 tart apples (e.g. Granny
  Smith), plus slices
  to serve
1 ripe mango
1 handful of spinach
1 tbsp sesame seeds

Special equipment
blender

Wash the apples, cut into eighths, and remove the core. Peel the mango, remove the pit, and roughly chop the flesh. Wash and shake dry the spinach. Put all the ingredients apart from the sesame seeds into a powerful blender with $^1/_2$ cup plus 1 tablespoon of water and blend until the smoothie has a creamy consistency. If necessary, add a little more water. Serve with apple slices and the sesame seeds sprinkled on top.

Lassi, a yogurt-based drink offered with almost every meal in India, is designed to offset the spiciness of the food. Traditionally, mango is used to add a fruity flavor to this drink, but here we have used a combination of apple and mint.

Apple and mint lassi

Serves about 4
Preparation 10 minutes

2 large sweet and tangy
  apples (e.g. Idared,
  McIntosh)
2 sprigs of mint, plus extra
  for garnish (optional)
1 handful of spinach
2 tbsp granulated sugar
1¼ cups full-fat yogurt

Special equipment
blender

Wash the apples, slice into eighths, and remove the core. Wash and shake dry the mint and spinach. Pick the mint leaves off the stalks. Put the apple pieces, mint leaves, and spinach into a blender with 1¼ cups of water, sugar, and yogurt, and blend until the lassi has a creamy consistency.

Decant into glasses and garnish each one with a sprig of mint, if using.

When the first winter frost covers the fields and meadows and the last few leaves have fallen from the trees, we love to make ourselves cozy at home with a glass of this apple punch. It's not too sweet, and it warms you up beautifully from the inside without any alcohol.

Apple punch

Serves 4
Preparation 15 minutes

½ cup (50g) cranberries
1 organic lemon
1 apple (e.g. Golden
    Delicious, McIntosh)
1¾ cups plus 2 tbsp apple
    juice
½ cup plus 2 tbsp cranberry
    juice
2 cinnamon sticks
3 apple tea bags (or 2½ cups
    plus 3 tbsp homemade
    apple tea, see p160)

Wash the cranberries, lemon, and apple. Slice the lemon. Core the apple and chop into small chunks. Halve the cranberries. Add the fruit to a large pan with the apple and cranberry juices plus $2^1/_2$ cups plus 3 tablespoons of water (or apple tea, if using). Add the cinnamon sticks and tea bags, if using, bring to a boil, remove from the stove, and leave to infuse for about 10 minutes. Pour into glasses and serve hot.

An apple (tea) a day keeps the doctor away: with more than 70 vitamins, nutrients, and trace elements, the apple is a super-healthy fruit that can help if you have a cold. This tea also contains calcium to help you get back on your feet if you're feeling exhausted.

Apple, star anise, and mint tea

Serves 4
Preparation 20 minutes

4 sprigs of mint
Scant 1oz (25g) dried apple
    chips (see p170)
2 star anise

Wash and shake dry the mint.
Add this to a teapot with the
apple chips and star anise. Pour
in $4^{1}/_{4}$ cups of boiling water.
Leave the tea to infuse for
10–15 minutes, pour, and enjoy.

PANTRY SUPPLIES

Homemade apple cider vinegar

Makes 2¾ pints (1.5 liters)
Preparation 10 minutes
Fermentation 6–8 weeks

2¼lb (1kg) organic apples
   or organic apple leftovers
   (skins and cores)
2 tbsp granulated sugar

Special equipment
2 sterilized 8½-cup glass
   containers
sterilized bottles

If you are using whole apples, wash them and chop into chunks. Take care not to include any rotten apples, otherwise there is a risk the vinegar will go bad. Put the apples in a large, sterilized 8¹/₂-cup glass container. Add the sugar to the apples. Top up with sufficient water to cover the fruit completely. Finally, put a clean cloth over the container to allow air to get in but protect the apple and water mixture against germs.

Leave in a warm place to ferment (ideally at about 77°F/25°C). The fermentation process produces a foam, which shows that everything is going well. To start with, the pieces of apple float on the surface. To keep them from getting moldy, stir the pieces into the liquid occasionally with a clean spoon.

After about 14 days, the pieces of apple will sink to the bottom and a mild vinegar aroma will develop. This means the first ferment is ready for the second stage of fermentation. By adding sugar to the apples at the start of fermentation, the process can be accelerated.

For the second fermentation phase, filter the first ferment through a cloth and decant the liquid into a second sterilized glass container. Once again, cover it with a cloth. The second fermentation takes between 4 and 6 weeks. During this period, a more intense vinegar smell will develop and the liquid will go cloudy. The vinegar should be tested regularly to see if it tastes as desired. As soon as it tastes right, you can filter it through a sieve and decant into sterilized bottles.

Tip: during fermentation, a cloudy sediment will develop that will later solidify and become gelatinous. This is the so-called vinegar "mother," a culture consisting of acetic acid bacteria. Do not throw this away; instead, add it to your next batch to speed up the production process. To store it, leave the vinegar "mother" in the vinegar in which it was grown. During storage, push it down from the surface into the jar from time to time.

With a little patience, you can use pieces of apple left over from cooking or baking to make cider vinegar. Depending on the sugar content of the apples you use, it can take 6 to 8 weeks to ferment your homemade vinegar. It's worth the wait. This vinegar is guaranteed to be free from any additives and, thanks to the apples, it contains lots of healthy nutrients.

This apple butter has nothing in common with conventional butter. It is much more like a thickly reduced apple sauce, and it is very popular. The apples are cooked at a low temperature until the sugar they contain has caramelized. The sweet and aromatic flavor goes beautifully with pork, and it also tastes fantastic spread on a slice of bread, in yogurt, or with waffles and pancakes. Depending on the variety of apples you use and your personal preference, you may need more or less sugar.

Apple butter

**Makes about 4 x 8fl oz/
½ pint (250ml) jars
Preparation 5–6 hours**

3lb 3oz (1.5kg) tart apples
    (e.g. Honeycrisp)
1lb 2oz (500g) sweet apples
    (e.g. Jonagold)
¾ cup brown sugar
3 cinnamon sticks
1 tsp cloves
1 vanilla bean

Special equipment
handheld blender
sterilized preserving jars
boiling-water canner
    (optional)

Peel, core, and roughly chop the apples. Put them in a pan with 2 cups of water and bring to a boil briefly. Cover and simmer over a moderate heat until the apples are soft. Stir regularly. Remove the apples from the pan, use a handheld blender to purée them, and return to the pan.

Add the sugar, cinnamon sticks, and cloves, and stir. Slice the vanilla bean in half lengthways. Scrape out the seeds with the back of a knife and add these to the purée along with the bean. Cover and simmer for 3–4 hours over a low heat, stirring occasionally. Over time, the color of the purée will gradually darken, the sugar will caramelize, and the mixture will thicken. Remove the lid and simmer the purée for a further 50–60 minutes.

Remove the spices and decant the hot apple butter into the sterilized jars. Seal tightly, invert the jars, and leave them upside down for 5 minutes. Turn them the right side up and leave to cool. Store in refrigerator.

To make the jars safe for unrefrigerated storage, process 10 minutes in a boiling-water canner.

We love granola—we eat it for breakfast and we use it as a topping for delicious desserts. The good thing about this recipe is that it contains no refined sugar. You can also tweak the ingredients in line with your personal preferences, substituting or adding oats, flakes, nuts, and dried fruit.

Apple and cinnamon granola

Makes 1 tray
Preparation 5 minutes
Cook 40 minutes

2¾ cups plus 2 tbsp rolled oats
1¼ cups plus 3 tbsp spelt flakes
½ cup plus 3 tbsp millet flakes
2 tbsp pecans
2 tbsp plus 1 tsp chia seeds
3 tbsp pumpkin seeds
1 tbsp plus 1 tsp sesame seeds
½–1 tsp ground cinnamon
½ tsp ground cardamom
¼ cup plus 1 tbsp neutral vegetable oil
¾ cup apple sauce or unsweetened apple purée (see p174)
¼ cup plus 1 tbsp maple syrup
3½oz (100g) dried apple chips (see p170)

Preheat the oven to 325°F (170°C). Combine all the dry ingredients except the apple chips in a bowl. Add the oil, apple sauce, and maple syrup, and mix everything thoroughly.

Spread the mixture out evenly over a baking sheet lined with parchment paper. Bake for 35–40 minutes until the mixture feels dry and is turning golden. Toss the ingredients about every 10 minutes. Remove from the oven, leave to cool, and add the apple chips. If preferred, you can chop up the apple chips first. Store in an airtight container and consume within a few weeks.

Thinly slice some apples and pop them in the oven. Homemade apple chips are a healthy snack requiring some time but minimal effort. We like to use different apple varieties for these dried rings. The tastier the apples, the more aromatic and flavorful the apple chips will be.

Oven-baked apple chips

Makes about 1¾oz (50g)
Preparation 10 minutes
Drying 4 hours

juice of ½ lemon
about 3 medium apples
    (e.g. Pink Lady, Idared,
    McIntosh, Jonagold)

Preheat the oven to 200°F (100°C). Mix the lemon juice with about $6^{1}/_{3}$–$8^{1}/_{2}$ cups of water in a bowl.

Wash the apples and remove the core (using an apple corer if preferred). Cut the apples into $^{1}/_{16}$–$^{1}/_{8}$in- (2–3mm-) thick slices. Place each one in the lemon water until you have sliced all the apples.

Line two baking sheets with parchment paper. Take the apples out of the lemon water and dab them dry. Place them side by side (not overlapping) on the baking sheets. Slide the baking sheets into the oven and prop the oven door open using the handle of a wooden spoon to allow any moisture to escape. Leave to dry for about 4 hours, rotating the baking sheets regularly in the oven.

The drying time will vary depending on the type and size of the apples. To test, take an apple chip from the oven and leave it to cool. If it is still too soft, leave the apple chips to continue drying.

Once ready, pack the apple chips into airtight containers and store in a cool, dry, dark place. They will keep for several months stored this way.

When we were children, we loved the smell of freshly cooked applesauce. The comforting scent of apples, cinnamon, vanilla, or cardamom would waft through every room in the house. Today, we still prefer our homemade applesauce, made without any refined sugar. If you have a sweet tooth, you can choose to use a sweeter type of apple. Our favorite is a combination of tart Honeycrisp with sweeter Jonagold apples.

Applesauce

Makes 2 x 16fl oz/1 pint (500ml) jars
Preparation 40 minutes

4½lb (2kg) tart and/or sweet apples (e.g. Honeycrisp, Jonagold)
juice of 1 lemon
1 vanilla bean
2 cinnamon sticks
½ tsp cardamom pods

Special equipment
handheld blender
sterilized preserving jars
boiling-water canner

Wash, quarter, and core the apples. Chop them into cubes and toss in the lemon juice. Slice the vanilla bean in half lengthways and scrape out the seeds.

Put $^3/_4$–1 cup of water, the cinnamon sticks, vanilla seeds and bean, cardamom, and apple in a large pan and bring to a boil. Cover and simmer over medium heat for 20 minutes.

Remove the vanilla bean, cardamom, and cinnamon sticks, and use a blender to purée the mixture. Return briefly to a boil before decanting into sterilized preserving jars. Process 20 minutes in a boiling-water canner. If preferred, you could also freeze batches of the applesauce.

Homemade apple jelly is a classic store cupboard ingredient. We like to use tart apples that are not completely ripe for this jelly because they contain more pectin, which helps set the jelly. This is a great way to use up windfalls from your garden.

Apple and ginger jelly

Makes 4 x 8fl oz/½ pint (250ml) jars
Preparation 2 hours

3lb 3oz (1.5kg) apples
    (e.g. Idared, Honeycrisp, Northern Spy)
3½oz (100g) fresh ginger
juice of 1 lemon
1–2 star anise
pinch of ground cardamom
1 tsp ground cinnamon
2 cups granulated sugar plus 2 tbsp pectin

Special equipment
sterilized preserving jars
boiling-water canner

Wash the apples and chop into small pieces, including the skins and cores. Put them in a pan with 2½–3 cups of water. The apple pieces should be completely covered with water. Bring to a boil and simmer over a moderate heat for 40 minutes without stirring.

Leave to strain for about 1 hour (or overnight) through a fine sieve lined with damp muslin or cloth. Do not squeeze the apples during this process, otherwise the jelly will be cloudy. Measure the liquid obtained in a jug. You need about 4¼ cups. If you don't have enough of this apple juice, top it up with some water (see also Tip, right).

Peel the ginger and chop into small pieces. Add this to the apple juice with the lemon juice and spices in a pan. Bring to the boil and simmer for about 5 minutes. Strain through a sieve. Set aside the star anise.

Stir the granulated sugar, pectin, and strained juice together in a pan. Bring to a boil over a high heat, stirring constantly, and cook at a rolling boil for at least 3 minutes. Add the star anise and transfer the hot jelly into sterilized jars. Seal tightly and process in a boiling-water canner for 10 minutes. Stored in a cool, dark, dry place, the jelly will keep for about a year.

Tip: you could also make this jelly by using 4¼ cups of store-bought apple juice.

You can serve our apple and onion chutney with meat or fish, in a sandwich, or with a burger: it is guaranteed to liven up even the simplest of meals. This chutney is tangy and sweet, slightly spicy, and packed with flavor. We like to eat it with cheese or as a delicious condiment for our wild boar burger (see p52).

Apple and onion chutney

Makes 2 x 8fl oz/½ pint (275ml) jars
Preparation 40 minutes

4 sweet and tangy apples, 1lb 2oz–1lb 5oz (500–600g) in total (e.g. Pink Lady, Cortland, McIntosh)
2 red onions
2 garlic cloves
½oz (15g) ginger
2 chiles
1 cup light brown sugar
1 tsp coriander seeds, crushed
¼ cup plus 3 tbsp raisins
½ tsp freshly ground black pepper
1–1½ tsp salt
½ cup plus 2 tbsp apple juice
½ cup plus 2 tbsp cider vinegar (see p164)

Special equipment
sterilized preserving jars (optional)
boiling-water canner (optional)

Wash and core the apples, peel the onions, and cube both ingredients finely. Peel the garlic and ginger, and finely chop both along with the chiles.

Put all the ingredients in a pan and stir. Simmer uncovered over medium heat for about 25–30 minutes, stirring regularly, until scarcely any liquid is left. The final consistency should be similar to jam.

Consume within 2–3 days. Alternatively, while the chutney is still hot, put it into sterilized preserving jars and process in a boiling-water canner for 10 minutes. Store in a cool, dark place for up to 3 months.

Our grandparents were experts when it came to preserving. Fruit and vegetables from the garden would be decanted into jars and preserved by cooking in a boiling-water canner. As kids we remember being treated to preserved pears, apples, and zucchini, many months after harvesting. And today we are still passionate about preserving. We love to eat our apples in vanilla with rice pudding, waffles, or pancakes.

Preserved vanilla apples

Makes 5 x 8fl oz/½ pint (250ml) jars
Preparation 50 minutes

3 tbsp lemon juice
3lb 3oz (1.5kg) apples (e.g. Cortland)
2 vanilla beans
¼ cup plus 2 tbsp granulated sugar
¼ cup Calvados (apple brandy)

Special equipment
sterilized preserving jars
boiling-water canner

Preheat the oven to 350°F (175°C).

Mix the lemon juice with $4^1/_4$ cups of water in a bowl. Peel, quarter, and core the apples. Remove any bruised sections. Place the apple segments in the bowl with the lemon water to prevent them from turning brown. Strain through a sieve, retaining the lemon water in a pan. Slice the vanilla beans in half and split them lengthways. Add them to the lemon water with the sugar and Calvados, and bring to a boil. Simmer for about 5 minutes.

Arrange the apples so they are densely packed in sterilized jars. Pour over the liquid and add ½ vanilla bean to each jar. Seal the jars and place them in a boiling-water canner. Process for 10 minutes. Remove and let cool.

The apples will keep for several months in the sealed jars.

This sweet tomato jam with chunks of apple is a fantastic companion for fish, and it also tastes great with strong cheese. We like to spread it on homemade bread (see p126) and eat it on its own.

Tomato and apple jam

Makes 2 x 8fl oz ½ pint (250ml) jars
Preparation 30 minutes

9oz (250g) cherry tomatoes
1 apple, about 3½oz (100g) (e.g.Jonagold)
1 small onion
2 tbsp balsamic vinegar
3 tbsp plus 2 tsp granulated sugar
salt and freshly ground black pepper

Special equipment
sterilized preserving jars (optional)
boiling-water canner (optional)

Put the tomatoes in boiling water and simmer until the skins begin to split. Plunge in cold water, peel, and chop roughly.

Wash and finely cube the apple. Peel and roughly chop the onion. Put the apple, onion, and tomatoes in a pan. Fry briefly. After about 5 minutes, add the balsamic vinegar, ½ cup plus 2 tablespoons of water, and sugar. Simmer for 15 minutes and season with salt and pepper.

Consume within 2–3 days. Alternatively, while the jam is still hot, put it into sterilized preserving jars and process for 10 minutes in a boiling-water canner. Stored in a cool, dark place, the jam will keep for 6 months or more.

In Korea, kimchi is served as a side dish with every main meal, and this tangy, spicy, fermented cabbage dish is becoming increasingly popular in Western countries too. Just like sauerkraut, kimchi uses lactobacilli bacteria to ferment the vegetables, thus preserving them. As well as having a unique flavor, kimchi is exceptionally healthy: it is rich in fiber and vitamins, and the large quantities of microorganisms it contains help maintain healthy gut flora.

Apple and green cabbage kimchi

**Makes about 4 x 16fl oz/
1 pint (500ml) jars**
Preparation 30 minutes
Stand 2 hours
Rest 4–7 days

2¼lb (1kg) green cabbage
¼ cup plus 1 tbsp coarse sea
    salt, plus extra if needed
2 tbsp fish sauce
1 tbsp rice flour
¾oz (20g) ginger
2 garlic cloves
2 small sweet and tangy
    apples (e.g. Pink Lady,
    Idared, McIntosh,
    Jonagold)
3 tbsp gochugaru (Korean
    chili powder, available in
    well-stocked Asian stores
    or online)
2 tbsp soy sauce
2 tsp salt
7oz (200g) radishes
7oz (200g) carrots
1 bunch of scallions

Special equipment
food processor
sterilized preserving jars

Remove the outer leaves from the cabbage. Divide the cabbage into eight pieces, then chop into bite-sized chunks. Add these to a large container and mix with the sea salt. Leave to stand for at least 2 hours (or overnight in the refrigerator). Then rinse thoroughly under running water and leave to drain completely.

Bring ¼ cup plus 3 tablespoons of water and the fish sauce to a boil, stir in the rice flour and simmer for 5 minutes. Peel and roughly chop the ginger and garlic. Peel, quarter, and core the apples. Roughly chop one apple. Purée the other apple in a food processor with the simmered fish sauce, gochugaru, ginger, garlic, soy sauce, and salt.

Peel the radish and carrots, and chop into cubes or strips, as preferred. Wash the scallions and slice into rings.

Mix the apples and vegetables thoroughly with the marinade in a large bowl. Transfer into sterilized jars, pressing the vegetables down well. Take care to ensure everything is covered in liquid. If necessary, top off the jars with some salt water.

Cover the jars—with plates, for example—and leave to ferment at room temperature for 4–7 days, depending on your taste. Check regularly to ensure the kimchi is covered with sufficient liquid. Finally, seal the jars tightly and transfer to the refrigerator. Open the jars occasionally during the first few days to allow any gases to escape. If any mold forms on the kimchi while it is fermenting, just scrape it off. The kimchi underneath is still good to eat.

Index

INDEX

Acknowledgments

Authors' acknowledgments

Although it is our names on the front cover—we are not
the only people who have worked on this special book.
We would like to thank everyone who has helped us
produce it. Special credit must go to DK Verlag for
giving us this opportunity and believing in us. To the
Hammerschmidt family, who not only showed us
their "Pomarium Anglicum" but helped us appreciate
the incredible number of apple varieties. How wonderful
that people like this exist: people who are so dedicated
to ensuring older varieties of apples are not forgotten.

Finally, we would like to offer special thanks to our friend
Moritz Hochhauser. He helped us with lots of delicious
cooking and contributed to recipe development.

Publisher acknowledgments

DK would like to thank John Friend for proofreading,
Vanessa Bird for indexing, and Kate Ramos, US Consultant.

DK LONDON

Translator Alison Tunley
Senior Editor Dawn Titmus
Editorial Assistant Lucy Philpott
US Editors Sharon Lucas, Lori Hand
Senior Designer Glenda Fisher
Managing Editor Ruth O'Rourke
Managing Art Editor Christine Keilty
Production Editor David Almond
Production Controller Rebecca Parton
Senior Jacket Designer Nicola Powling
Jacket Coordinator Lucy Philpott
Art Director Maxine Pedliham
Publishing Director Katie Cowan

DK DELHI

CTS Designer Umesh Singh Rawat
Pre-production Manager Sunil Sharma

DK GERMANY

Recipes, text, and photographs Madeleine and Florian Ankner
Cover photo Madeleine and Florian Ankner
Editorial Margarethe Brunner
Internal design, typography, implementation, cover design Atelier Schug: Sibylle Schug, Astrid Shemilt, Barbara Mally
Program management Monika Schlitzer
Editorial management Anne Heinel
Project support Jessica Kleppel, Julia Sommer
Production management Dorothee Whittaker
Production control Ksenia Lebedeva
Production Verena Marquart, Sabine Hüttenkofer

First American Edition, 2021
Published in the United States by DK Publishing
1450 Broadway, Suite 801, New York, NY 10018

Copyright © 2021 Dorling Kindersley Limited
DK, a Division of Penguin Random House LLC
21 22 23 24 25   10 9 8 7 6 5 4 3 2 1
001–322910–Aug/2021

A catalog record for this book is available from the Library of Congress.
ISBN 978-0-7440-3377-9

DK books are available at special discounts when purchased in bulk for sales promotions, premiums, fund-raising, or educational use. For details, contact: DK Publishing Special Markets, 1450 Broadway, Suite 801, New York, NY 10018 SpecialSales@dk.com

Printed and bound in China

For the curious

www.dk.com

NOTES

Recipes: the butter used in the recipes is unsalted.
Tip: don't throw away apple peel or cores; instead, use these in other recipes, such as cider vinegar (see p164), for instance.

The information and suggestions in this book have been carefully considered and checked by the authors and publisher, however, no guarantee is assumed. Neither the authors nor the publisher and its representatives are liable for any personal, material, or financial damage.

This book was made with Forest Stewardship Council ™ certified paper—one small step in DK's commitment to a sustainable future.

For more information go to www.dk.com/our-green-pledge